For:

An outstanding girl in
a remarkable time!
Love,
Grandpa Pat

SOMEWHERE IN THE NORTHWEST *2005*

On the Road in Oregon & Washington

Patrick C. Wilkins

Bear Creek
Press

SOMEWHERE IN THE NORTHWEST

ON THE ROAD IN OREGON & WASHINGTON

ARTWORK ("Sasquatch," page 52) BY
Frank Tuning of Wilder, Idaho

PUBLISHED BY
Bear Creek Press
814 Couch Avenue • Wallowa, Oregon 97885
541-886-9020 • bearcreekpress@eoni.com
www.bearcreekpress.com

PRINTING HISTORY
Bear Creek Press First Edition, July 2004

FRONT COVER
Cedar Creek grist mill (Woodland, Washington) by Patrick C. Wilkins

Printed in the United States of America.

ISBN: 1-930111-46-0

World Headquarters located in Wallowa, Oregon U.S.A.
(at the old Abbie Riggle place on Bear Creek Road).

AUTHOR'S NOTE

S erious news has almost always been at the top of any news broadcast. And that's all followed by other stuff. The sports, the weather, maybe how the stock market is doing, an oddity or two. And then the kicker, a human interest story whose purpose is to leave 'em laughing. Or if not laughing, at least appreciating something other than mayhem.

For years and years as a television on-the-road reporter, that was my specialty, giving people the last laugh. I must confess, I did it purposely to give them— and me, too—relief from all the terribly serious parts of life aired just before. And while it was an exacting job, it was always interesting and often downright fun.

Pat Wilkins (left) on the road with cameraman Don Stapleton

To own up, most of the stories in this book are veterans of TV, radio, and newspapers. That is, they previously have been either seen, heard, or read because I discovered and reported them for those media. Yet they have remained, well, evergreen. Like the Northwest. The reason they are here, out of the thousands of stories I've covered, is that they are some of my favorites, and I'd like to share them with you for the same reason I did them in the first place.

One more thing: A friend and former co-worker not long ago asked me how I would describe today's news formula. I replied that it's still the same as it was, except the language has changed. "If it bleeds, it leads" was once an old jest and now a lamentable fact. Another is "If it laughs, it's last." But, fortunately, this is still an excellent position for what we all like best—having the last laugh.

Patrick C. Wilkins

LIST OF PHOTOGRAPHERS

SAGEBRUSH SANDALS, THE BIGGEST SMALL PARK, BRIDGE OF THE GODS, BIG RED, PIONEER APPLE TREE, WEATHER GOATS, GRIST MILL CELEBRATES, WORST FOOD RESTAURANT: Pat Wilkins

THE LAST FLUME: Courtesy Cam Thomas, Broughton Lumber Company

TYPEWRITER ARTIST: Clif Wilkins

WHOSE TRAIL?: Courtesy Polk County Museum, Rickreall, Oregon

OREGON BOY'S INVISIBLE PLANE: Courtesy U.S. Defense Department

GRAND COULEE DAM LAMPLIGHTER: Rod Egbert collection

NUTTY NARROWS: Pat Wilkins; Tim Johnston, courtesy Cowlitz County Washington PUD

OREGON, MY OREGON: Anastasia Buchanan; Buchanan family collection

TOM'S TOMB: Stan Killingsworth

THE BATTLE OF HARRY'S RIDGE: Roger Werth, courtesy *The Daily News*, Longview, Washington

CROWS FOR THE HANDICAPPED: Courtesy *The Register-Guard*, Eugene, Oregon

THE TOILETS FLUSHED BACKWARDS: Sunny Speidel; the Photography Collection of Suzzallo Library, University of Washington

FOR LOVE OF A BARN: Pat Wilkins; Selander family collection

OREGON OR BUST: Wilkins family collection

TABLE OF CONTENTS

FOREWORD

When I got my first job in television, working as a part-time film editor at Portland's ABC station, I soon found myself working side by side with people I'd watched on television for years. One of them may not have been widely known outside the twenty-fifth largest market in the U.S., but he was a bona fide news icon in my hometown. Pat Wilkins was a longtime, well-respected local anchorman, the newscaster who thousands of Northwest viewers turned to for their nightly dose of information.

Over time we became good friends. I overcame being awestruck at working with someone so well known, partly because Pat proved to be a regular guy who treated me more like a colleague than the rookie I was. As I moved up and became an on-air reporter, he offered advice about how to improve my stories, and never failed to congratulate me on those rare occasions when I actually told a story well.

Pat was also my boss for a period, but never seemed comfortable as the news director. He was more journalist than administrator, a newsroom iconoclast who was inclined to challenge rather than do the bidding of the station's front office.

We frequently discussed such things over drinks in the bar across the street, gabbing about the good and bad of our industry and the stories we were working on.

"I'll have no more than one more," I recall Pat deadpanning repeatedly as he ordered another round, the hour late but neither of us wanting the conversation to end.

Eventually, he resigned as boss and even quit anchoring. Pat wanted to return to his first love, feature reporting, which didn't make much sense to me since I was still thrilled by covering "hard" news, chasing cops and fire trucks. But in the ensuing years, I marveled at watching Pat do what he does best: traveling the back roads and telling the stories of real people, real places and the many wonderful things other reporters seemed to miss.

His story work was so compelling that ultimately I also felt the call to leave the "bad" news behind in favor of covering feature subjects exclusively. By now I, too, have reported on thousands of them, though undoubtedly not as well as Pat.

He is, in short, a fine storyteller, which is about the highest compliment you can pay to anyone who strives to work in words, either broadcast or print.

What follows is a collection of his best, and I envy you if you're about to experience Pat's stories for the first time.

If you find yourself reading too late into the night, unable to ignore what the next chapter might bring, I suggest you sit back, relax, and follow Pat's advice—have no more than one more.

– Paul Linnman, television news anchor and reporter, radio show host, and author of
The Exploding Whale: And Other Remarkable Stories from the Evening News

SAGEBRUSH SANDALS

C an it be that the sun-baked high desert country of eastern Oregon was home to humans more than 13,000 years ago? Discoveries made at Fort Rock Cave certainly make it seem so. And if so, who were these people?

Fort Rock itself is the remains of an ancient volcano. The forces that molded the mass, which probably sprang up through the waters of what was then a huge lake, did the work more than 10,000 years ago. And in that frame of time, the event may have been witnessed by people who have long since vanished but who, scientists say, lived in the area as long ago as 13,000 years. The evidence has been found in many places in the region. But perhaps

the most dramatic, and certainly the most important, discovery was made just a mile from Fort Rock at a place called Fort Rock Cave.

An early explorer of the cave in the 1930s was Dr. Luther Cressman, who pioneered and developed the University

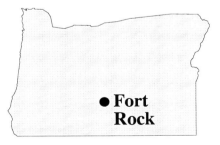

● **Fort Rock**

Fort Rock

of Oregon's anthropology department. Dr. Cressman liked to joke that his fifteen minutes of fame came from the fact that he was the first husband of world-renowned anthropologist Margaret Meade. But the truth is, of course, that Cressman gained a wealth of celebrity for his own work. Some of the most important of that work was unlocking the secrets of Fort Rock Cave.

In the 1960s, this cave became the most celebrated of the ancient human-occupied sites in the region when between seventy-five and one hundred sagebrush sandals were found there. The discovery captured the public's fancy. But more important to science was the excavation of fire hearths at several levels. One was 6,000 years old; deeper yet was one dating back 10,000 years. And then came the payoff: On the very floor of the cave, Cressman found a hearth that he carbon-dated to 13,200 years ago.

If Dr. Cressman were working today, he may be part of a lively debate over new theories that suggest southern and eastern Asians and Europeans migrated to the North American continent well ahead of the Asian Mongoloid people who crossed the Bering Strait on a land bridge about 11,500 years ago and then wandered into Alaska. New digs have turned up old bones that do not fit the features of American Indians, as well as tools that date back more than 15,000 years, a time we'd previously assumed was too early for people to inhabit America.

What we do know is that when the Fort Rock people, these *first* Oregonians, lived in their cave, it overlooked a lake. It was a time of mammoths and mastodons, camels and bisons that shared the grounds. In

Fort Rock, as seen from the cave

and around the lake were flamingos and waterfowl, even fish that resembled today's salmon.

Today, sagebrush instead of water extends from the cave entrance and rolls to the horizon. A ranch stands comfortably in easy sight. But modern explorers can still find obsidian chips, hold them in their hands and, for a fleeting moment, look though the eyes of the people who once lived here…at Fort Rock Cave.

THE BIGGEST SMALL PARK

Dick Fagan and Patrick O'Toole had something in common. They were both leprechauns. Fagan, though, passed himself off as a reporter for Portland's *Oregon Journal* newspaper, and he wrote a lot about O'Toole, passing him off as the resident-in-residence of a little plot of land right on the waterfront road of Portland's Front Avenue.

Originally this spot on Front caught Fagan's gaze because his part of the *Journal's* office overlooked a hole in the ground. Legend has it that the hole was to have received a light pole. But instead, the hole received weeds, lots of weeds. Weeds came and came and clogged the two-foot space, and so Fagan, enchanted by his Irish luck of having survived service in World War II, one day saw Patrick O'Toole standing in those weeds. O'Toole waved, it seems, and said something like, "We are kin," giving license to Fagan to fantasize about founding in Portland the only leprechaun colony west of Ireland. Fagan destroyed the weeds and planted flowers, actions

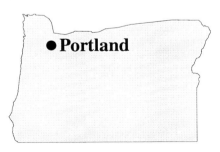

that prompted O'Toole to support Fagan's vision. O'Toole stayed on and Fagan stayed daydreaming.

Fagan was a very good writer about odds and ends of things he bunched into a column called "Mill Ends." His scrutiny of real things and situations and reporting about his observations of such, though much read and liked, were challenged in popularity by his whimsy. His biggest whimsy became the world's smallest park. Mill Ends Park.

That hole in the ground sprouted wings, became a haven for butterflies who loved, according to Fagan, to dive off their own little diving board into a tiny pool.

Only Fagan could see Paddy (Patrick) O'Toole, the head leprechaun, though Paddy allowed *anyone* to see the other sprites of the colony. But because most people couldn't see them, either, Dick kept his readers apprised of the goings-on in the park. It was a big task because leprechauns cavort a lot—after all, they're Irish, you know—but Dick Fagan imagined we'd all be interested in the frolic. He was right.

And so for twenty-two years he wrote about events in Mill Ends Park. Not every day, mind you, but often enough that we knew what was happening in this western frontier outpost of Ireland, a place that was tiny and macadam-locked, but still important.

Then in 1969, not long after Fagan had joined a bunch of journalists touring eastern Oregon—after viewing the old gold strike ghost towns, the developing ski areas, the fantastic and remote holdings of actors Walter Brennan and Eugene Pallett, the sweeping and enchanting views of wide open spaces with their exhilarating emotional pull—Dick died. Of cancer.

Mill Ends Park had lost its founder. But not its voice.

In 1976 the city of Portland, mindful that the Guinness book of records is always scooping up best, biggest *and* smallest, assumed maintenance of Fagan's creation. It became a Portland city park. It is to this day. Located on what is now the Naito Parkway (formerly Front) and Taylor.

Both the *Oregon Journal* and its building from which Fagan looked down are long gone. But the park remains.

So on St. Patrick's Day I don my Kelly-green corduroy shirt and drive to Portland, cruise down what is now Naito Parkway, and slow down as much as I can while

Mill Ends Park

passing Mill Ends Park. I'm always hoping to catch a glimpse of Patrick O'Toole. I never do. But I always see the spirit of Dick Fagan.

WASHINGTON PIONEERS
GEORGE W. BUSH AND GEORGE WASHINGTON

George W. Bush and George Washington had a lot in common. First of all, both were named for the first president of the United States, were strong advocates of freedom, and were among the earliest of Oregon Trail emigrants, so were prominent figures in opening the West. One other thing—both were black. Yes, George Washington and George Washington Bush were a lot alike.

Even their births were similar. Bush was born free in Pennsylvania, son of a black sailor and, it's said, an Irish housemaid, and was raised by a wealthy Quaker ship owner.

Washington was born in Virginia, also of a black-white liaison, his father a black slave, his mother a white servant. Washington, like Bush, was further raised by family friends. And eventually, both wound up in Missouri.

George Bush

Along the way, however, their fortunes differed greatly, having to do largely, it can be presumed, from their early disparate circumstances. Bush being reared in a realm of wealth, became a prosperous merchant-farmer, while Washington grew up in a wealth of struggle and found it difficult to make a living.

But both shared another thing in common—a fear of what was then the status of blacks in America. The state of Missouri was half-slave and half-free, and while both Bush and Washington were technically freemen, they became fed up with their situations in a state rife with slavery tensions and severe laws imposed on blacks. They packed up and joined wagon trains headed for Oregon: Bush in 1844 and Washington in 1850. They, like so many other people of the time, were home-hungry and looking westward to the Oregon country with its promise to fill that need. Both, however, were sorely disappointed.

After long months of soul-searing travel on the Oregon Trail, they arrived in the territory only to learn the freedom they sought was as elusive as it had been back east. The Oregon provisional government, though inclined to be anti-slavery, had not only outlawed the holding of slaves, but also prohibited "Negroes" from residence in Oregon. What a blow! To have come nearly two thousand weary miles only to find that those repressive anti-black laws, which they thought they'd left behind forever in Missouri, had caught up to them in this pleasant new land—Oregon.

But both Bush and Washington had plenty of pluck. Bush and his family, along with some friends who'd also made the journey, swung north across the Columbia River into what was to become the state of Washington. He was assured of being safer there, out of reach of the exclusionary law because at the time the British controlled the area north of the Columbia. Bush's group settled in the area of what was called Tumwater, very near what is now the state capital, Olympia. Bush got ownership of his 640-acre claim, "Bush Prairie," via special petition.

He built a good life for himself and his wife and five children on the new frontier. Unfortunately, he did not live to see passage in 1868 of the 13th and 14th Constitutional Amendments giving him, and all blacks, full citizenship.

George Washington's luck took a turn for the better when he staked a squatter's claim on land at the confluence of the Skookumchuck and Chehalis rivers. While the law said he could not own land in the Northwest, the friends who raised him, James and Anna Cochran, moved onto his homestead and proved it up for the required number of years, then deeded it to Washington. Finally, Washington started to prosper.

In the early 1870s Washington and his first wife, Mary Jane, platted a town of four square blocks they named Centerville. That was the beginning of the village today known as the city of Centralia, Washington.

George Washington

Washington is credited with using his own money to "nurse" the fledgling burg through panics and other hard times, and with helping many other settlers to survive by finding them employment and low-cost land. Today's citizens have immortalized the man with an enormous image of Washington painted on one of Centralia's largest buildings.

Of course, Washington State was named for the first president of the United States. But you might also like to think, as I do, that it was named for a couple of Oregon Trail pioneers.

BRIDGE OF THE GODS

Indian legends have a way of keeping the truth alive. And that is certainly true about the story of the Bridge of the Gods, the fabled natural arch said to have spanned the Columbia River in prehistoric times. Oral history and scientific investigation agree that in the hundreds of years prior to the white man's coming, there was a place where Indians could cross the great river without getting their feet wet. They called this place "Wauna." Science and legend part company only on the cause and form of the bridge. And even then, they are not far apart.

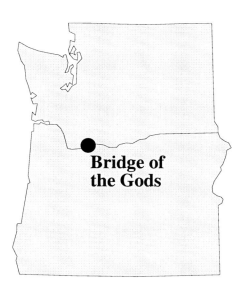

Bridge of the Gods

Scientists tell us that about a thousand years ago, half a mountain on the north side of the river fell into the stream and blocked its flow, probably the result of seismic activity. Indian

The Bridge of the Gods today

legend tells us it was the work of the Great Spirit. The cataclysmic event occurred along a stretch of the river where Bonneville Dam now stands, along with the present-day towns of Stevenson, Washington, and Cascade Locks, Oregon. The blockage created a lake that probably was larger than the backwater pool of Bonneville, and drowned forests for miles and miles upstream.

Logic has it that the earthen dam was continually eroded until it finally washed out, leaving an expanse of dangerous cascading rapids. Legend has it, however, that the enormous current of the breakthrough of the lake tunneled under the south-side range, leaving in its wake a solid rock and earth span high above the flow. A bridge. And, of course, it was created by the Great Spirit.

For as long as the bridge stood, it was tended by an old crone called Loowit. Legend is not quite clear on what her duties were. Maybe she took tolls. Perhaps she was a bridge inspector. At any rate she was there for centuries, until a couple of the Great Spirit's sons, Klickitat (Mt. Adams) and Wy'east (Mt. Hood), got to fighting over a woman (Squaw Mountain).

Loo-wit tried in vain to stop the war of rocks and fire. The whole world shook and the bridge collapsed into the rapids, carrying the devoted attendant to her death. Her dedication, however, was rewarded by the Great Spirit. He put life back into her, set her up as the young, lively beauty we know as Mount St. Helens. No fiction here, only legend and maybe the truth.

The most famous likeness of the bridge was imagined by the late Indian artist Jimmie James, whose 1960s charcoal drawing of it is always part of any Cascade Locks promotion of the Bridge of the Gods. James, who is buried at Cascade Locks Cemetery, once said he had "hard-hat" dived on the

Jimmie James' Bridge of the Gods

reach of the Columbia where the bridge supposedly stood. "The pattern of rock strewn along the bottom," he said, "convinced me the bridge did exist."

There is a Bridge of the Gods even today: a modern steel span first built in 1926 and then raised to a position above the dam's reservoir when Bonneville Dam was constructed in 1938. Oh yes—soon after flying solo across the Atlantic in 1927 and then barnstorming across the country, the "Lone Eagle" Charles Lindbergh flew *under* the span as a lark. It was a spur-of-the-moment stunt that caught Gorge dwellers by surprise. But they must have agreed the fleeting act was a tight fit.

Nowadays, the bridge is owned by the Port of Cascade Locks and has an attendant twenty-four hours a day, seven days a week. Toll takers they are, with names such as Patty Joe, Valerie, Jean, Rose, Dorothy, Ronnie, Jeff, and Kenny. But if you know the legend, you think of them as...Loo-wit.

Sir Francis Drake in Oregon

Would you believe that Sir Francis Drake has an Oregon connection? Well, some people think so and would like others to believe it, too. About twenty years ago, one of these believers set out to convince us that Drake spent more than a month in the summer of 1579 at Whale Cove on the Oregon coast.

But why would he have tarried there? After all, he was on the final leg of his around-the-world plunder cruise. This was Drake the privateer, the freebooter, the scourge who ransacked Spanish treasure ships along the way, the Drake whose ship was laden with booty that ultimately would make him, his crew, his Queen, and his nation rich.

He was on his way home, so why stop at Whale Cove?

Well, because after long months at sea, his ship, the Golden Hind, was badly in need of repairs. To make those repairs, the crew would have to *careen* the vessel. That is, turn it on its side to scrape off

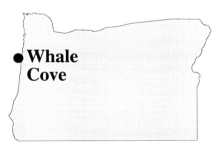

Sir Francis Drake

barnacles, re-caulk leaking seams, and replace rotting wood. Whale Cove is a small harbor, but in those days of tiny ships, Drake might have found it a perfect place to do the job.

But most theories have Drake doing his ship repairs in a bay near San Francisco, his "Port of New England," prior to his sailing farther west and completing his circumnavigation of the globe. But in the summer of 1985 an English engineer, writer, and historian by the name of Robert Ward thought he had nailed down Whale Cove as the spot of the Hind's repairs. This countryman of Drake's even came to Oregon to twist the arm of conviction.

To promote Whale Cove as Drake's Port of New England, Ward produced two ancient maps published some time after Drake's voyage. They perfectly match Whale Cove, one of them so closely that it shows a small jut of land, the cove's peninsula, in two parts, depicting its appearance at both low and high tides. Ward also said the description of a single animal gives substance to Whale Cove as the ship repair spot: the muskrat, native to the Oregon coast. A perfect map, a perfect animal. But not proof.

An archaeological dig was also done in 1985, but it produced no hard evidence of any European presence, not a single relic connected to Drake. The probe did discover refuse piles and human remains high on cliffs above the cove, at a place believed to have been a seasonal Indian camp dating back about five hundred years ago. In other words, the Indians would have been there at the cove when Drake was there—*if* he was there.

The Golden Hind

This 1550 map, one of the first ever drawn of the Western Hemisphere,
shows the difficulties mariners such as Sir Francis Drake faced in navigating the globe.

Then cruising along the Oregon coast in the summer of 1987, there came
a ship that looked for all the world like the Golden Hind. Its crew, wearing
sixteenth-century sailors' duds, could have been mistaken for Drake's crew.
The boat carried the name "Golden Hinde," spelled with an "e" at the end, as
the English of Drake's time might have spelled it, but with a "II" added. Yes,
it was a replica of the English commander's ship. And whatever else the
Golden Hinde II did that summer, it was important to Bob Ward, who wanted
the ship to prove that Drake could have easily sailed into Whale Cove. The
new Hinde people were glad to give it a try.

But the boat was at the mercy of capricious winds and arrived at Whale Cove before high tide. So it did not sail in, could not sail in. The seamen took a look, shook their heads, and sailed on.

Everyone there seemed satisfied that it could be done, so Drake could have done it. But did he? Even if the replica Hinde had made it into Whale Cove, the question would remain: Was Drake really here in the summer of 1579?

BIG RED

Before Big Red drifted into town, Scio, Oregon, had long boasted that it was the "Covered Bridge Capital" of the western United States. This despite the fact that the little Linn County community has no covered bridge of its own. Oh, it does have a bridge all right, one smack in the middle of town that spans Thomas Creek—but it doesn't have a roof. Scio, however, is the *hub* of a cluster of covered bridges for miles around. So the self-proclaimed fame is warranted.

But ever since a big Rhode Island Red rooster hopped off a pickup truck in May of 1999 and began panhandling for handouts, the hamlet has not been the same. People in Scio, you see, detected right away that this was no ordinary rooster. He was big and handsome, and strutted as if he were the very chicken who crossed the road to show the possum it could be done without becoming road kill.

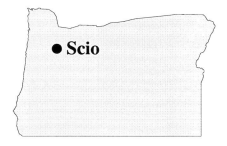

Big Red and some Scio friends

Feed Store owners Audie and Marian Heikkila were so impressed they offered him their place to roost at night. He showed his trustworthiness by not eating up the profits, although he once set off the burglar alarm.

School kids, merchants on Main Street, regulars like the bread truck delivery guy, and visitors passing through on their way to covered bridges also fell victim to the chicken's charm. He just had to have a name, so they called him "Big Red." Soon, very few mentioned that he was originally from Rhode Island, and they treated him like he were a Scio native.

Big Red returned their kindness by becoming the Grand Champion at the Linn County Fair just a couple of months after he arrived in town. That was followed by a flurry of publicity: Newspapers and TV stations, even CNN, did delightful stories about Red. All this attention on the bird focused a lot of attention on Scio, too, with the result there was less and less talk about covered bridges, and more and more about "the town rooster."

Nevertheless, it looked to some that Red was intolerant of outsiders, although he had come from elsewhere himself. One day a group of wild turkeys, maybe five or six, strolled into town, and Red ran them off. Or did he? Veterinarian Sally Cole says it was more likely he was running after the turkeys because he thought his harem had arrived. Either way, territorial imperative or simply amour, the turkeys skeedaddled back to the wild.

But there was more. Taking time from his daily strolls along the length of Main Street to chinwag and snack with friends, Red posed for local artist Raven Okeefe, whose watercolors of the rooster generated a line of Big Red products ranging from T-shirts to mint tins to note cards. All this could have gone to Red's head, but it didn't. He was already cocky, so becoming ruler of the roost couldn't change his personality all that much. He was, in a word, self-confident. The people of the town liked that a lot. They liked his celebrity even more.

Still, celebrity can bring unwanted attention. We don't know if it was jealousy or what, but a couple of times Red was stalked by a dog—a dog who then actually *chased* him to the point where Red had to take refuge and hide underneath a car. The stalking stopped, though, when the animal's owner, a fan of Big Red's, placed her dog under house arrest.

And then early in 2004 came the death of antique shop owner Carol Bates, Red's best friend. She and he used to sit chatting on a bench in front of the store, each seeming to understand the other's language. It was Carol who once said she'd never seen Big Red attempt to cross the street. But maybe that was because Red had never seen any possums to help. And since she's gone, Red's often at her door.

But there's no one who can explain to him that no matter how loud he crows, his friend Carol will not come outside.

THE LAST FLUME

It seemed as if the Broughton Lumber Company's lumber flume would go on forever. After all, it was built in 1913 and it was now 1986, and there was comfort in knowing that what was believed to be "the last working flume" in the country was still doing a tremendous job. Besides that, the nine-mile-long water chute was historic, a holdover from the turn into the twentieth century. It was both venerable and invulnerable.

Since the beginning, the flume tapped the Little White Salmon River for water to do its work. Its job had always been to float rough-sawed lumber (cants) the nine miles from Broughton's mill in Willard, Washington, to the edge of the Columbia River: first through huge stands of Douglas Fir forest, and then along the face of the Columbia Gorge, where mile-after-mile of the flume clung to rock cliffs in full view of passing motorists on both sides of the river.

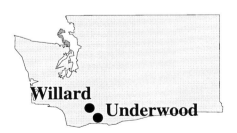

In short order, the downward pitch of the structure delivered the "goods" to the company's re-saw and shipping facilities at river's edge near Underwood, Washington. And because it held on so long, this dinosaur of old time logging and lumbering won widespread attention from movie producers and TV reporters.

One of the more fun things to do was to put people and cameras in the flume inspection boat, building plots around the flume for both drama and just plain amusement. Nationwide audiences saw the flume in such productions as the movie *Charlie, the Cougar* as well as in the long-running television series that starred that lovable Collie, Lassie.

Legend has it, too, that some courageous (or foolhardy) timberman would sometimes jump aboard a cant and attempt to ride it the length of the cascading water. Because it's mostly word-of-mouth, the record is unclear whether anyone ever made it all the way from mill to mill. It was dangerous, too, because sometimes the lumber would jam up, tripping a system that dumped the water from the chute, but maybe not in time to save a cant jockey from rushing to disaster. Thus, it can be presumed that the company probably discouraged such activity.

From time to time the flume was hit by wildfire and rock slides. Of course, those damaged sections were quickly repaired. Its history and its function made the flume a wonderful structure.

But in the late summer of 1986, Broughton announced that for economic reasons it would close its Willard mill and dismantle the flume. What a shock! To the hundred or so laid off workers and to those sightseers who often visited the flume.

Most news reports at the time made much of the structure's history. So somehow it seemed important, and certainly ironic, that in the flume's final days workmen made new repairs to it, striving to keep it patched and working until the very end.

That end came in December of the same year. The flume, however, was given the chance to live on as a museum piece—or pieces—at some of the region's historic storehouses.

Broughton removed some sections for reasons of safety and liability, but some of it was also cut into sections for display in Portland and at a logging museum on the Oregon coast. But most of the portion seen from both Columbia River highways in the Gorge was left standing for the benefit of the newly curious and those already in the know.

Slides, perhaps fire, and certainly decay and brush now advance to wreck and consume it. That comes as a jolt to those amongst us who thought the flume would be here forever.

LEWIS & CLARK DOG

Historians sometimes make captivating discoveries that change the record and set it straight. Take that big, black, male Newfoundland dog that was a member of the Lewis and Clark Expedition. Until recently the name of Meriwether Lewis' dog was sort of a multiple choice guessing game. That was because ink has a tendency to run, but more to blame was the unruly and independent spelling of members of the trek who kept journals.

Captain Lewis purchased the animal in either Philadelphia or Pittsburgh, shortly before shoving off from Pittsburgh on the early first leg of the journey of exploration which was to take the Corps through unknown country and Indian tribes to the Pacific Ocean and back.

Some writers have romanticized the dog's role on the journey. And that is perhaps fitting because he established himself as an important asset, proving to be a tenacious hunter and just as resolute as a watchdog, a sentry, if you will.

Newfoundlands are huge. So as far as Newfoundlands go, Lewis' dog was doggone big, probably weighed between 130 and 150 pounds. Also, guided by the appearance of today's Newfoundland breed, he was handsome, with a coat of long, dark hair. And since he was just growing into adulthood, young and bristling with muscle, he displayed much enthusiasm for his part in the adventure.

Early on, the Lewis and Clark dog exhibited his talent for being a provider, running down and killing squirrels, goslings, rabbits, grouse, and other small game and, apparently, never once devouring them on the spot, but always bringing them to Lewis or other members of the party for the communal pot.

More important, he was also good at bagging bigger game. Both Lewis and Clark as well as Sgt. John Ordway tell in their journals about several instances involving deer: once, when the big Newfoundland chased one into the river, drowned it, and pulled it to shore; another, when he ran down one with a gunshot-broken leg and finished it off; and still another, when he chased one, overtook it, and dragged it down. Yes, this dog was an extraordinary hunter.

As a sentinel, he was just as zealous. In the middle of one night a buffalo bull charged through camp, coming within inches of the heads of sleeping men, then making a beeline straight for the tent of Lewis and Clark. The dog leapt to the challenge, and his barking, snarling, and teeth-gnashing caused the bull to swerve aside, avoiding the injuring or even killing of the expedition leaders.

On the other hand, his eagerness as watchdog was sometimes overplayed. In grizzly country, for example, he was prone to stay up all night, howling the alert against prowling bears. You can imagine this probably kept many of the men awake all night, else his incessant yowling would not be so much recorded in the journals.

The dog and Captain Lewis had something in common—both were wounded. The dog was bitten by a beaver, and Lewis was accidentally shot by a member of the party who mistook him for an elk. Both injuries were to legs. Actually, in Lewis' case it was more likely his buttocks. The dog almost died. Lewis, though mighty uncomfortable, didn't lapse that far.

Lewis' affection for his animal was apparent in his outrage when the dog was stolen by Indians near the Columbia River Cascades. He sent a three-man party in pursuit of the thieves, with orders to shoot to kill if that was necessary to retrieve him. It was one of only a few times during the entire expedition that Lewis issued such a command directed at Indians. The dog was recovered, though, without a shot being fired.

Meriwether Lewis

The dog made the entire trip from east to west and back again, and his celebrity is such that today there are numerous Newfoundland dog clubs across the land. Many owners have named their dogs "Scannon" after Lewis' dog. But that was *not* his name.

In their journals, Lewis and Clark referred to him only as "my dog" or "our dog." Sergeant John Ordway, in his journal, gave him a name that appears to be "Scammon" or "Scannon," depending on how one sees Ordway's freestyle spelling, or how the ink ran.

Until about 1988, writers seemed to favor either of those names. A children's novel in 1959 by Adrian Stoutenberg and Laura Nelson Baker was called *Scannon: Lewis and Clark's Dog*. In a 1968 book titled *Meriwether Lewis*, author Richard Dillion refers to the dog as "Scammon." No less an authority than the National Geographic Society published a volume in 1970 named *In the Footsteps of Lewis and Clark*. Its writer, Gerald Snyder, went with "Scannon."

Historian Donald Jackson, who at the time was Professor of History at the University of Virginia, wrote a fine foreword to that book. But years later, Jackson, a researcher in great detail, stumbled across the fact that on the return trip, Lewis had named a small tributary of the Blackfoot River near what is now Missoula, Montana, "Seaman's Creek." S-E-A-M-A-N. Seaman.

Subsequent searches of the original Lewis and Clark journals did find a field note by Lewis with the clear spelling. Not Scannon, not Scammon, but Seaman. Consequently, all writers of recent histories of the Corps of Discovery, including the 1996 publication of Stephen Ambrose's acclaimed *Undaunted Courage*, call Seaman by his real name.

Unfortunately, the name did not stick to the creek. Some years after Seaman passed through, it was renamed for an early French trapper. The stream is now known as Monture Creek.

ABRAHAM LINCOLN
OREGON GOVERNOR

It's hard to imagine Abraham Lincoln as governor of Oregon in view of what we all know about the sixteenth President of the United States. Yet the Great Emancipator, the man who freed the slaves, earlier in his career had the chance to govern the Oregon Territory back in 1849. All he had to do was accept the appointment to that post from newly elected President Zachary Taylor. He refused.

Today it's a guessing game as to why Lincoln didn't come to Oregon. But it's fun to speculate about that as well as what his life and politics would have been like if he had accepted the job. Obviously, his political career and life would have taken a much different route. And the history of the United States and Oregon would be much different from what it is today.

As a U. S. congressman from Illinois, Lincoln was a staunch supporter of, and campaigner for, Taylor during the 1848 presidential campaign. It is curious that this anti-slavery representative, but perhaps not yet resolute abolitionist, so strongly supported the candidacy of a slave-owning military

Abraham Lincoln

man who had never voted, and who was a hero of the Mexican war, which Lincoln adamantly opposed. It seems, however, that he was willing to exploit the popularity of the man called "Old Rough-and-Ready" into a Whig party presidential victory.

What Lincoln *really* wanted from Taylor was to be appointed Commissioner of the General Land Office, an important sub-cabinet post under the Department of Interior. He lost out.

The next post offered Lincoln was that of *secretary* of the Oregon Territory. He did not consider that post-election reward as anything but demeaning.

Taylor took Lincoln's discontent to heart and quickly offered him the *governorship* of the Oregon Territory. Now that was a prestigious position—overseer of a vast developing region, a post that would certainly enhance future political ambition. But Lincoln declined.

Why? Well, that's part of the guessing game. So let's enlist the help of retired U. S. Senator Mark Hatfield, who also served two terms as Oregon governor. Hatfield is a Lincoln scholar of the first order and a practitioner of independent thought—a characteristic that coincidentally, and perhaps ironically, links Lincoln and Hatfield in a number of ways. Perhaps the most dramatic example is Lincoln's opposition to the Mexican War and Hatfield's vanguard opposition to the Vietnam War, each position occurring at a time when such a stand was unpopular.

Hatfield has said that if Lincoln had come to Oregon, he would have had a profound effect on the growing pro-slavery mood in the territory. "Oregon was filled with antagonists to a central government telling them what to do," Hatfield says, "an attitude fostered by the then-Governor Joseph Lane, a pro-slavery North Carolinian, appointed by President Polk."

Lincoln would have replaced Lane, and Hatfield believes Lincoln, who was "a strong believer in a central government," would have injected his views with the result that he would have "defused the pro-slavery attitude" in the territory.

It was fortunate, however, that Lincoln did not come to Oregon. For it was during this critical period that the Republican party was formed, with Lincoln as one of its principal founders. "But for the presidential candidacy and victory of Lincoln in 1860," Hatfield claims, "Oregon and California would have seceded from the Union."

Lincoln carried both states. It was a turning point, too, for Joseph Lane, the former territorial governor and the first U. S. senator from Oregon, when the territory was granted statehood in 1859. Lincoln's victory had the effect of ending Lane's political career.

But really, why *did* Abe Lincoln shun Oregon? Anger about the Land Office-Oregon Secretary-Oregon Governor shuffle? Possibly. Some historians, however, are sure it was because he was reluctant to leave a secure political base he had built with much labor and time in Illinois. But there might have been an even more compelling reason.

His wife said, "No!"

Mary Todd Lincoln, it is thought, had no enthusiasm for sailing around Cape Horn, going to an unsettled frontier with a family that included a seriously ailing three-year-old son. (You'll remember Eddie Lincoln did not live to age four.) So, that's it—Mrs. Lincoln put her foot down. No Oregon!

And boy, was the future President lucky to have had his wife refuse the Oregon job. President Taylor served only a year and a half before he died, presumably from eating spoiled cherries. Vice-President Millard Fillmore would have stepped up and, at least in Hatfield's view, Lincoln probably would have been replaced by someone closer to the new President. Then what would Lincoln have done? The guessing game continues.

There would have been a couple of options: either return to Illinois and refurbish his political base there, or stay in Oregon and attempt to set up a law practice. Hatfield believes that if he had gone back to Illinois, Lincoln may still have won the presidency.

On the other hand, what would have happened had he stayed in Oregon? "Abraham Lincoln," Hatfield says, "would be someone we've never heard of!"

HOMER OF SILVERTON

There was a time in Silverton, Oregon, when, if you sighted just right, you could line up Homer Davenport's tombstone with the big, old grain elevator a block away, making it look like the gray of the tin-coated elevator was an extension of Davenport's marker. But the elevator was torn down to make way for new low-level buildings and a parking lot.

Not that Homer needed such an extension. His stone is pretty big, anyway. And that's because in life Davenport was pretty big, too. That is, he was important. He was considered to be one of the best, if not *the* best, political cartoonists of his time.

Not only that, but Homer is also noted for bringing the first Arabian horses to this country in 1906, an adventure he turned into a book. He also penned *The Country Boy,* a volume in which he glowingly recounted the days of his youth, growing up in the rolling Waldo Hills farmland near Silverton.

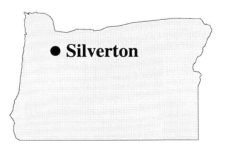

Homer Davenport
1867–1912

Davenport was at the peak of his career working for the Hearst newspapers in New York, fighting crime and waging political influence with his cartoons, when the Titanic sank. He was dispatched to cover the tragedy. He was ill but still eager to lend his drawings to illustrate the calamity. But his affliction turned into pneumonia and he died. He was just forty-four years old.

And so the folks of Silverton have always been proud of Homer, both alive and doing his work, and dead, keeping the town alive.

You see, although Davenport lies in the little town's cemetery plot, in company with a number of his pioneer relatives and friends and admirers, he gets resurrected the first week in August every year. "Homer Davenport Days," they call it. It's a celebration.

Silverton has never forgotten the hometown hero because he never forgot the town, even when his fame spread worldwide, and he hobnobbed with the likes of President Teddy Roosevelt. The memory of Homer Davenport is not dimmed but probably only enhanced by new attractions such as the sprawling, gorgeous, ever-growing Oregon Garden in Silverton. But most of all, a man's character can be judged a great deal by what he says about his hometown and his dog.

He said much the same about both, but his tribute to the place of his birth leaves no doubt that, from his lofty position, the internationally acclaimed cartoonist always longed for home.

"The strangest part of Silverton is that it never releases me a day from its hold," Davenport lovingly wrote in the preface to *The Country Boy*.

A Homer Davenport cartoon

"I have thought of it while seated in the ruins of the Colosseum at Rome, thought of it in London and Paris and Constantinople, thought of it while resting in a death-like silence of the shadow of the Sphinx, and told of it near the Euphrates River in Arabia, while among the wild tribes of Anezeh.

"I shall never desert Silverton; it is my home and always will be."

That's love! And the town reciprocates that love to this day.

Homer Davenport's
portrait of his father, 1894

Silverton, Oregon 1908

49

Sasquatch's Agent

What do Marilyn Monroe, Elvis Presley, and Sasquatch have in common? Roy Craft, that's what! Maybe you'd like to know why? Well…

Marilyn and Elvis's publicity agent sat there in the tiny newspaper office, dragging deeply off his third or fourth chain-smoked cigarette, taking little notice of where the ashes fell. He didn't have to; he owned the place, bought with money he'd made promoting Monroe and Presley and other stars in the "good old days."

Roy Craft had abandoned Hollywood to live at Stevenson, Washington, where he bought the *Skamania County Pioneer*, a small weekly newspaper in a little town in the magnificently large and picturesque Columbia River Gorge. Marilyn and Elvis were in the distant past. Yet Craft couldn't let his public relations skills go to waste, so he took on another well-known client. His name was Sasquatch. Yeah—Bigfoot.

Not that Bigfoot had hired Craft, but more like Roy had the idea that Bigfoot

An artist's depiction of Sasquatch

could be made into a star. A really big star! So Craft latched onto Sasquatch as the beast's promoter and the leader in Bigfoot security. Craft was of the mind that even if you didn't believe in Bigfoot, you were always on the lookout for him. And so reported sightings of the big guy, of course, helped Craft sell newspapers. Trouble was, reported sightings were not proof.

Some believers in Bigfoot thought the best way to prove his existence was to find one and bag him—that is, shoot him—and bring him in draped over the hood of a pickup. But Roy Craft, used to working with sensitive people like Marilyn and Elvis, was appalled. No one is going to murder Sasquatch on my watch, was his attitude. And so he leapt to the forefront in Bigfoot's defense.

Meanwhile, Bigfoot scurried around the Gorge like a terrified six-point buck deer during hunting season, leaving giant tracks for the Skamania County Sheriff's Department to cast in plaster of Paris. There was a flurry of sightings. It was rumored Bigfoot was worth three-million dollars—dead or alive.

Hunters with big rifles thought the odds better than taking a shot at the lottery. They came, searching for the tracks. Those rumors, however, broke the back of any sort of resistance to legislation for the protection of Sasquatch, especially from those people who thought the whole thing was silly.

Sasquatch security had to be had. Say some tourist was wandering around out there in the woods, and one of those Bigfoot bounty hunters mistook him for Sasquatch. Craft was quick to point out, both privately and publicly, that the possibility of a vacationer being mistakenly blown away by some hair-triggered nut made it imperative that Sasquatch be protected so the general public would be protected as well. This gave rise to the classifying of two possible types of Sasquatches: Type A (hairy), apparently meaning wild, and Type B (hairless), meaning domestic. If you shot either, you were in trouble. If Bigfoot were to attack you, that was another matter; self-defense would be a strong argument, if Bigfoot wound up dead in such a confrontation.

So in 1969 Bigfoot was guaranteed sanctuary in Skamania County, Washington. And while Marilyn Monroe, Elvis Presley, and Roy Craft since then have all passed on, Bigfoot—Sasquatch—is still alive. Thanks to his agent.

Oregon Trail Tunes

W hat sort of music do you think came along with pioneers on the Oregon Trail? The late Ron Brentano used to ask himself that question a lot, and then he set about finding the answer.

Brentano was a musician, artist, and composer who worked for the Oregon Historical Society in Portland, and attempting to learn what kind of music Oregon Trail pioneers played and sang—and yes, even composed—was for years his favorite project. He found that songs popular on the trail were those popular all over the East at the time. Interestingly, many of those tunes are still familiar today.

That being said, Ron Brentano was always delightfully surprised whenever he turned up a "today" song that actually stemmed from the time of the big western migration to the Oregon Territory. Among the durable music Ron found was "Red Wing," "Arkansas Traveler," "Sourwood Mountain," "Oh Susannah," and "Bonaparte's Retreat," the latter of which was a big, smash, pop hit in modern times.

So what the pioneers brought with them was music popular at the time: some written by Stephen Foster, and others performed by minstrel bands.

"It's amazing," Brentano said. "They're still with us in spite of music changes, in spite of rock & roll and everything else."

Songs actually composed by pioneers on the trail have not fared so well. Brentano took on an enormous task, going through pioneers' diaries and looking for direct references to music. Some led to tunes he found music for and so learned to play. And while the songs deserved documentation, Brentano said they were much too slow and sentimental for today's tastes, such as the tunes "Camping on the Mountain" and "Farewell."

Farewell's the word that breaks my heart,
and fills my soul with woe.
But the fertile fields of Oregon,
encourage me to go.

See?

"…the evening meal is just over. Near the river a violin makes lively music, and some youths improvise a dance; in another quarter a flute whispers its lament to the deepening night."

— Jesse Applegate, 1843

Musicians in Aurora, near the end of the Oregon Trail

Ron figured the more popular tunes on the Oregon Trail were those that people could dance to; music that, in Brentano's words, "provided entertainment at the end of a long, hard day." And so a person with a banjo or fiddle was one of the most important members of a wagon train.

Ron's own banjo was from the 1840s, a handmade instrument that had no frets, just inlaid ivory guides, and strung with catgut strings. His flying fingers picked that five-string relic for years: bluegrass, jazz, country, and his own compositions such as "Bonneville Rag," "Willamette Falls," and, of course, his special tribute to his adopted state and his response to his wife's question about the weather: "It's Raining Again."

Brentano found that old banjo in Seattle in the 1960s, but he always said he liked to believe it came west on the Oregon Trail. If it did, its owner then must have strummed some of the same songs that are played yet today, here at the end of the Oregon Trail.

CHIEF PAULINA'S DEATH

The place where Shoshone War Chief Paulina died in 1867 has become a modern-day crime scene. A guy by the name of Allen Jacobs , a retired Oregon State Police crime scene investigator, has made it so. But from the Indians' perspective, the remote central Oregon area now known as the Paulina Basin—and specifically the spot where Paulina was killed, near what is today Ashwood—has *always* been a crime scene. In fact, most whites of the time considered the whole *region* to be a crime scene, not because a couple of them bushwhacked Paulina, but because the far-ranging Shoshone warrior chief had killed so many of them.

Even today, Jacobs is so convinced that Paulina was such a cold-blooded renegade killer that in comparison, he says, "Crazy Horse [a principal leader of Indian forces that wiped out the Custer command at Little Bighorn] was a Sunday school teacher."

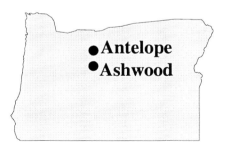

Chief Paulina

Still, Jacobs has done his investigation of the spot where Paulina was killed as meticulously as he would of any murder scene. It appears the work is a retirement hobby, but downright serious, nonetheless, and may tie up a loose end or two that have flapped in the wind of history.

There's no argument that Paulina—which translates to "The War Spirit"—was good at what he did during the Shoshone campaign in and around the Ochoco. What he did was kill, burn, and pillage. His followers often rode horses stolen in raids against the whites, and he frequently fed his people with stolen beef. His was a name cursed by the military sent to wipe him out.

Of course, Paulina was just one of many Indian leaders set against the whites in a war that lasted from 1863 to 1868. It must be noted, too, that other Indian tribes jumped in on the side of the whites, and the Shoshone took vengeance on these people as well.

It was near the end of April of 1868 when Paulina and his band wrapped up a successful rampage that included raids in Jordan Valley, the Pueblo Mountains, Harney Basin, and Mormon Basin. In the final days of the forays and with only a few remaining braves, Paulina struck two ranches and a stage coach station very near home. About twelve miles south from the stage stop near today's Antelope, the warriors camped and treated themselves to a meal consisting of a cow slaughtered from among the herd they had just driven off. That was a big mistake, stopping to eat.

Station attendant Howard Maupin, stage driver Jim Clark, and a tag-along passenger trailed the Indians to their encampment and shot Paulina and killed one other raider. The other Indians broke and ran. Seeing the end—and to avoid the possibility of being scalped with his own knife, a disgrace above all other humiliations for a Shoshone—Paulina drove his knife into the ground and twisted it to snap its blade. Initially, Paulina had been felled by rifle shots. He was finished off with pistols.

It was in 1996 that Allen Jacobs and friend Loyd Greenwade searched the site of Paulina's death and found slugs that were probably those that had passed through his body. Using metal detectors, Jacobs found more bullets and several shell casings of the size Maupin and Clark would have used.

A faint buzz of the detector at one spot could have been ignored, but not by this dedicated crime investigator. Jacobs dug down three inches and found the remnant of a knife blade. But only the tip and barely over an inch long. A knife that fit the point perfectly was found a short distance away. It was bent at the hilt, testifying to Paulina's attempt to break it. Jacobs says that after failing to crack the knife, the dying Indian simply threw it away, as far as he could.

A good thing, too. For although the knife is now a rusty relic with the handle rotted away, on April 25th, 1867, it could have still been used to lift a scalp.

Chief Paulina *was* scalped. But not with his own knife.

Typewriter Artist

The Rose Haven Nursing Center in Roseburg, Oregon, is the home of artist Paul Smith. It is also his studio. Paul is not a Rembrandt or a Picasso. But friends believe that in his own way, he might be even better. Paul, you see, "paints" with a typewriter. And while Rembrandt Harmenszoon van Ryn and Pablo Picasso had great control of their bodies to do their work, Paul Smith does not. He was born with spastic paralysis, a condition that causes continuous muscle spasms.

Paul painting with a typewriter is a wonder, all the more a wonder because of that condition. He trembles and twitches and shakes—sometimes uncontrollably. He struggles to talk, to make himself understood. Yet his works of art range from portraits of presidents and popes to animals and landscapes, and reproductions of such famous works as the Last Supper and the Mona Lisa. Many are in color; all are done with one laborious peck after another on the typewriter keys.

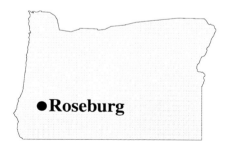

●**Roseburg**

Paul Smith

But what a struggle. It's not like Paul has Parkinson's, a tremor disease that has afflicted the likes of former U.S. Attorney General Janet Reno and actors Katharine Hepburn and Michael J. Fox. No. He really has something different. He has to fight. His left hand grasps the right hand to steady it, or maybe to steady both. It often takes several tries, but finally his right index finger strikes the right key. And there's another mark in a piece that might take weeks or months to complete.

"The pictures themselves were astounding enough just being done on a typewriter," said John Cermak, a friend who first saw Paul's work thirty years ago. "But when I saw who did it, I was floored. It was incredible!"

Before Cermak died, he was a big promoter of Paul's art, trying for years to find a patron to support Smith's work so the typewriter artist could make a living and leave the nursing home. There were no takers.

I first met Paul on his sixty-eighth birthday, and by then he had already come far and done well for someone who doctors thought wouldn't last a week when he was born in 1921. At that initial meeting, he was struggling with a self-imposed deadline, putting the finishing touches on a portrait of his friend, hairdresser Charlotte Fleming. It was to be her birthday present. In a precious moment, Charlotte cried as she took the gift of her likeness from Paul's typewriter.

"I'll put this on the wall of my beauty shop," she squeezed out through sniffles. "So the whole world can see."

Some of the whole world has seen Paul's art. His portraits have gone to such high places as the White House and the Vatican. Former President Bill Clinton sent Paul a nice note thanking him for a portrait Paul did of him.

Other famous people respond in kind. One of Paul's most treasured mementos is a letter from Mother Teresa sent from Calcutta, India. It was in response to a letter sent by friend John Cermak in which he included some of Paul's work, one of which was a portrait of the renowned missionary worker.

Smith's Mother Teresa, created on a typewriter

Mother Teresa wrote that she and her Sisters were "deeply moved" by the art, and added "You are an inspiration and an example to all of us."

For as long as he lives, Paul is determined to continue to work, and he laments only that despite his skill on the typewriter, he has never been able to control his spasms enough to write anyone a letter of his own.

PIONEER APPLE TREE

There is an Oregon pioneer that, despite all odds, has survived to this day, and now lives in the state of Washington, having put down roots in what was known as the Oregon Country close to two centuries ago.

Most of the pioneers who came to the Oregon Territory were farmers from the Midwest's farm country. Even those who were not farmers had to take it up because they had to eat. Promise of agriculture in the territory proved true. A mild climate and a long growing season, aided by omnipotent and ubiquitous rain, developed farming into a major part of Oregon's economy. And it has remained so. One of those plants of bountiful harvest, predating even the Oregon Trail, is alive and still in good health.

It's even more noteworthy because it has not only withstood time and triumphed over weather, but also resisted the onslaught of modern civilization. Ironically, human beings are responsible for both its survival and the constant threat to its life.

Fort
Vancouver

Fort Vancouver, 1845, from a sketch by Lt. Henry James Warre of the British army

This great Northwest survivor is an apple tree, the lone remnant of an orchard planted at the Hudson's Bay Company's Fort Vancouver in 1825. Yes, a tree that rooted in Dr. John McLoughlin's compound on the Columbia River almost two decades before the big influx of emigrants trekked the Oregon Trail. The tree's track record includes having survived such catastrophes as the 1894 flood, the notion to cut it down in 1910, the Columbus Day wind storm of 1962, and many ice storms. Obviously, it has lived a long time—more than twice the span of the average human life.

But in the early 1980s, it faced its biggest threat ever—the construction of a freeway interchange. The venerable tree was in the way and had to give ground to concrete. There was some thought of moving the famed monarch, but Washington highway landscape designer, Dave Rodin, had another idea— nudge progress over just a bit so the freeway ramp would edge by the tree. And so that's where it stands today, along Washington Highway 14, at a spot where its branches overlook the current Interstate 5 freeway interchange, just off the north end of the Interstate bridge that crosses the Columbia River between Vancouver and Portland.

The ramp building also spurred archeological digs at the site of a village that once stood just outside Fort Vancouver, a village of which the tree must have once been a part.

But the builders of the roadway didn't just surround the tree with a concrete maze and then steal away. No, it now resides in its own little park, landscaped to highlight its presence. And for better or worse—lets hope for better—the tree still blossoms and bears fruit.

So careful planning helped the tree survive another threat to its life. And with additional care and pruning, we're told, Dr. McLoughlin's tree should live for another hundred years. Meanwhile, it is to be admired as a landmark as famous for its amazing survival as for its longevity.

The pioneer apple tree today, standing near an Interstate 5 bridge

Sacajawea's Son

If Meriwether Lewis and William Clark had had their druthers, they'd probably have chosen not to take an infant along on their expedition of discovery to the Far West. But they had no choice. So Jean Baptiste Charbonneau became the youngest member of the Lewis and Clark party. As it turns out, it was fortuitous circumstance; both the baby's mother and the tot came to be of considerable importance to the band of explorers.

"Pompy," the baby was called, and his mama's Indian name was largely ignored, too, by the men of the Corps of Discovery. They called her "Janie." Pompy, often shortened to "Pomp," was much shorter and easier to say than Jean Baptiste. The nickname was probably first bestowed by Clark, the expedition's co-captain who loved the kid, doted on him, and gave him a name meant to signify his standing in the company.

And why was Jean Baptiste's mother called Janie? Well, her real name was either Sacajawea or Sacagawea or

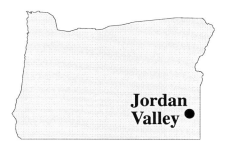

Jordan Valley •

Sakakawea, all Indian words that, depending on how you spell it, means either "Boat Launcher" or "Bird Woman." Bird Woman is today's most popular interpretation of Sacajawea's name, but Janie she was on the Lewis and Clark trek.

Pomp did not come into the world easily. His was a difficult birth. Most difficult! We have the word of William Clark about that. In writing. He described the coming out of Jean Baptiste as "tedious and pain violent." But one Indian suggested during Sacajawea's arduous labor that she take a potion made of water and a crushed rattle from a rattlesnake—and bingo! Only ten minutes after she gulped it down, the baby was delivered. Go figure.

Less than two months later, strapped to his mother's back, Jean Baptiste Charbonneau went along as a non-working member of the Corps of Discovery, heading into the wilds of the West and toward the Pacific Ocean. His mom went along as a sort of "package deal," in that Lewis had hired Sacajawea's husband Toussaint Charbonneau as a guide and interpreter. But she and her baby might have been of more worth than the husband.

Sacajawea spoke Hidatsa, learned from the tribe that stole her in a raid when she was just twelve years old, as well as her native Shoshone. Shoshones had horses, and her knowledge could assist in trading for them. But in one of those moments almost beyond belief, at a council with Shoshone leaders she suddenly recognized one of the chiefs: her brother! Incredible luck. And in the business of trading for horses, a tremendous edge.

Even if one doesn't accept the legend of Sacajawea as a brilliant guide (after all, she was only fifteen or sixteen years old at the time), one should accept the fact that she and her baby were a stabilizing influence on the men of the Corps of Discovery and, as Clark put it, a valuable "token of peace" among the Indians.

Sacajawea died at the age of maybe twenty-two years old in what is now South Dakota, although the oral history of some Indians has it that she lived to be quite old, and along the way had a number of additional kids.

And what of Jean Baptiste—Pomp? William Clark became his guardian and saw to his education. Pomp spent six years in Europe, became fluent in English, German, French, and Spanish. He then spent nearly four decades roaming the Far West as a mountain man, gold prospector, interpreter, and guide.

He left the California gold fields for a new strike in Montana. Along the way he caught pneumonia and died on May 6, 1866, at age 61, at a remote southeast Oregon hostelry. His grave, now a National Historic Site, is about three miles off Highway 95, near Jordan Valley. This is the final resting place of Sacajawea's baby, the youngest member of the Lewis and Clark Expedition.

Jean Baptiste Charbonneau's grave outside Jordan Valley, Oregon. The epitaph on the plaque reads, "Under the wide and starry sky…"

WHOSE TRAIL?

Oregon pioneer Levi Scott has received a lot of recognition for his accomplishments. His name is attached to a town (Scottsburg on the Umpqua River), a valley (Scott's Valley, about midway between Salem and Grants Pass), and a mountain (Mt. Scott in Crater Lake National Park).

His name is also associated with the forging in 1846 of a southern route of the Oregon Trail that ran from Fort Hall, Idaho, to the Willamette Valley. In fact, he was one of the leaders of a party of fifteen men who blazed that wagon road. And therein lies the rub. The trail is called *Applegate*.

Brothers Jesse, Lindsay, and Charles Applegate were also early emigrants to the Oregon country, and their family name is attached to a lot of things, too: a town, a river, a lake, all in the southern part of the state. And Jesse Applegate, along with Levi Scott, was also a leader of the 1846 expedition that developed the southern route.

Levi Scott

It was Scott, however, who led the first wagon train that year along the undeveloped route from Fort Hall into Oregon, while Applegate went ahead with a group of men who were supposed to blaze the trail and clear its obstacles. In other words, they were to make a crude wagon road.

Jesse Applegate

Unfortunately, the advance party apparently did their work haphazardly or not at all, leaving Scott with the responsibility of having to recruit workers from amongst the travelers who would remove timber, brush, and rocks.

Scott was also alone in taking the barrage of criticism from the extremely dissatisfied emigrants—a few of whom, Scott was sure, were talking about hanging him. He didn't lose much sleep about it, though, because he was the only one who knew where they were and which way they had to go.

"If it were not for the tenacity, fortitude, strength, and dedication of Levi Scott," says Polk County, Oregon historian Arlie Holt, "the pioneers of those seventy-five wagons in that train could have suffered a fate similar to the infamous Donner party, trapped by winter and frozen to death."

Some of the best information about the Scott-led trek through the wilderness is contained in a manuscript of reminiscences attributed to the work of Scott. It does have his hand in it, such as, "The life and adventures of a backwoods orfent boy from his infacy to old age by him self."

But the real author of the compelling story of the journey, told in first person narrative as Levi Scott, was actually James Layton Collins, one of the emigrants Scott led to Oregon. Collins, only a boy at the time of the traversing of the southern route, became lettered and was later a lawyer and judge. The collaboration of Scott and Collins on the manuscript produced an absolutely

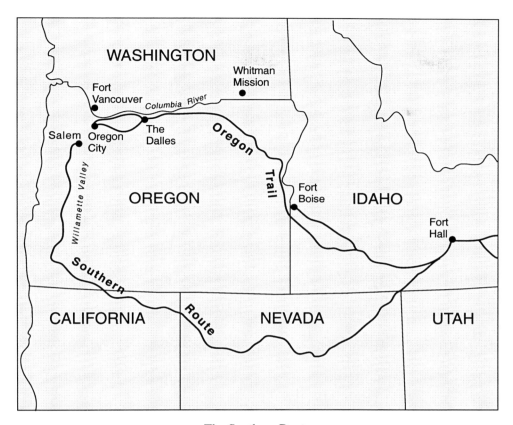

The Southern Route

fascinating record of pioneer times and, in particular, the worth of Scott in opening an alternate route to Oregon.

In short, Scott emerged as the commander and most important member of the 1846 venture. Some historians acknowledge that; others do not. And some latter-day Oregon Trail publicists have simply ignored him.

That fact has considerably irked historian Holt. Particularly irksome to Holt are those signs all along the way of the pioneer route that designate it as the Applegate Trail. Holt points out that those signs were promoted in 1946 to celebrate the centennial of the opening of the trail. Advocates of the Applegate appellation, who had already acquired the blessing of the Oregon Highway Commission to put up the signs, ignored opponents that included the Oregon Historical Society, which had ruled it was to be named the Southern Route. The signs were installed and that was that—the Applegate Trail.

In Holt's view, however, if the old course was not to be designated the Southern Route and named for the leaders who developed it, at the least it should be called the Applegate-Scott Trail. But more appropriately, he indicates, it should be known for the benefit of tourists and Oregonians alike as the Scott-Applegate Trail.

OREGON BOY'S INVISIBLE PLANE

The opening strike of the 2003 Iraqi war was dumped right on the roof of the "Butcher of Baghdad" in an attempt to lop off the head of the country's regime. Saddam Hussein was home, it's said, and "smart" bombs that swooped down from Stealth F-117A Fighter-Bombers were right on target. Unfortunately, the butcher's luck held for a while. He survived. Close—but no cigar.

We all know that the F-117 is one of the United States' major weapons engaged in the Iraq war. Most of us also know the Stealth has no need to sneak past enemy radar because radar can't "see" the plane. What many of us may not know is why our opponents cannot detect the Stealth. The reason is that a 1956 Dallas, Oregon, high school graduate came up with the aircraft design that makes the plane "invisible." He's called Mr. Stealth, this country boy from Polk County.

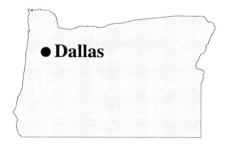

His real name is Denys Overholser, described in his high school year book as "Most Cooperative" and a guy who lettered as a member of the school's wrestling team. And let it be known in the self-appraisal portion for graduating seniors that his ambition was to "make a million dollars."

Jump ahead to the 1970s, the Cold War period of missile standoff between the U.S. and the Soviet Union. A time of tension. A time to develop additional tools of war and discover how to thwart radar's detection of those tools. And in particular, so far as Overholser's skills were concerned, how to fool radar, how to make a plane invisible and get ahead of the Russians. He did just that. It catapulted him from, in his words, "village idiot to village genius."

Denys Overholser, an unusually bright mathematician and radar specialist, worked at the time for the Lockheed-Martin Aircraft Company in Burbank, California, in a secret project building called the "Skunk Works," so named because of the awful odors that came from a nearby plastics factory. Ben Rich, the Skunk Works boss, says Overholser dropped into his office one day and presented him with "the Rosetta Stone breakthrough for stealth technology."

Ironically, that breakthrough was based on a theory authored by a Russian scientist. The Soviet designers were not interested in their own guy's work, but Overholser dug deep into it, as only a nerd's nerd would, and evolved his own concept of how to beat radar.

The answer was a dramatic, totally different design for a plane—a weird-looking craft of myriad triangular panels, joined together in such a way as to eliminate flat surfaces, like a cut diamond. It looked like an arrowhead. Tests proved it to be imperceptible to radar, the plane's image reduced to about the size of a ball bearing. The Stealth went into production and the rest, as they say, is history.

The Stealth planes played a big part in Desert Storm, the first conflict with Iraq back in 1991. And then again in the second war to oust Saddam Hussein. In subsequent documentaries seen on the History and Discovery

TV channels, Overholser is given due credit for the Stealth development. Pilots call him "Mr. Stealth" and praise his machine, if you'll excuse the cliché, to the high heavens.

As of this writing, Mr. Stealth has relatives who still live in Oregon, including his mother, Janice Overholser, who still resides in the old home place south of Dallas. Denys' own home these days is said to be somewhere in the Caribbean. And although his whereabouts is rather vague, unlike his plane he is *not* invisible. Sometimes his image pops up on TV when those documentaries are rerun to coincide with the second Iraq war.

And although we don't know for sure, it would seem his early ambition to make a million dollars has been fulfilled.

The Stealth F-117 Fighter-Bomber

GRAND COULEE DAM LAMPLIGHTER

The Grand Coulee Dam stretches across the Columbia River almost a mile from bank to bank. On a grand scale, the dam provides water to irrigate millions of acres of once-arid land, and generates electricity for industry and homes. So it seems strange that just *one person* was responsible for making sure the lights of the dam itself were lit.

The Grand Coulee Dam lamplighter was Rod Egbert, and he had a never ending duty. There are fourteen miles of tunnels—Rod calls them "galleries"—inside the dam, and it was Rod's job to scoot along the long, narrow corridors on an electric cart, replacing burnt out bulbs as he went. The stops were frequent, the tour continuous.

There are light bulbs everywhere inside Grand Coulee Dam, perhaps more fixtures, it seems, than in any of the tiny towns near this biggest of the great dams on the Columbia—Washington towns such as Grand Coulee, Elmer City, Belvedere, Nespelem, Coulee City, and

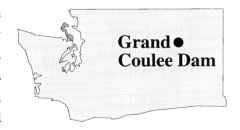

Grand Coulee Dam

Electric City. They were all well lighted, of course, but they had lots of lamplighters—mostly homeowners.

Egbert did the same kind of work they did whenever a bulb burned out, but on a grand scale. Unlike a homeowner, however, Rod had to anticipate how many lamps he might have to re-light on his rounds, and then load up his cart accordingly. He came to have a real feel for how many, and so his became a pretty efficient operation.

In the 1980s when Rod Egbert was first doing the lamplighting at Grand Coulee Dam, he explained that the tunnels are for providing access for maintenance work on the dam. So keeping them well lighted is essential.

The job also required a lot of legwork, which often carried him into areas where the passageways are little more than damp caves. Areas where the cart could not go. Areas where if you were claustrophobic, you would not go. Rod was not claustrophobic and welcomed the side-trips into the smaller, dank tentacles of the labyrinth as an opportunity to stretch his legs.

Back and forth and up and down went Egbert, eight hours a day, five days a week. Putting light bulbs in sockets all along the way, lighting the tunnels of the Grand Coulee Dam, a facility that in turn lit up much of the Northwest. But, ironically, because his job was a day-shift, Rod never saw the light of day. That was then, this is now.

Rod Egbert

Today, Rod's job is done by several people, a chore divided into sections and performed by various utility men. Rod no longer lamplights. Not to worry, though. Egbert still works at Grand Coulee, but is now a full-fledged electrician. That's because, in the words of public information officer Craig Sprinkle, "Rod has been one of our 'brighter' employees."

NUTTY NARROWS

S ome celebrities will do almost anything for publicity. But not Mickey Mouse. Not Chip 'n' Dale. They need something really special to which to lend their presence, something that might go international, make it worth Walt Disney's time. And his stars' time, too.

That's why Amos Peters and I were sitting out there in the hot sun, staring up at his bridge. It wasn't a big bridge, as bridges go; just sixty feet long and only six inches or so wide. Nutty Narrows, it was called, and was for the exclusive use of squirrels. A bridge of necessity to keep them safe. And we were waiting to see a crossing squirrel.

Amos Peters was a compassionate man. He was a Longview, Washington, building contractor, too, but his worth as a humanitarian emerged when he came up with the idea for the Nutty Narrows bridge. Peters was appalled by the constant slaughter of squirrels as they tried to cross the busy street just outside his office window. The clincher was when Amos found a dead squirrel with a

nut still in its mouth, squashed while simply trying to make a living. Something just had to be done to stop the carnage!

So Peters and some friends, with the blessing of the city, strung a tiny bridge made of cable, fire hose, aluminum, and wood high above the street. Some said it looked something like New York City's George Washington Bridge. Its looks, however, mattered little to the squirrels who were more interested in its utility. And very soon they caught on to this corridor, this safe pathway across Olympia Way. People were delighted to see the animals scurrying along the bridge and couldn't wait to report their sightings to the press.

That did it! News services picked up the Nutty Narrows story and spread it around the world. The contagion became contained after a time, sure, but it was all a great deal of fun while it lasted. And every once in a while, the story was revisited because Nutty Narrows was famous. One of those revisits by me was in 1970, about seven years after Peters built the span. I had learned

Nutty Narrows Bridge

the Longview squirrel population had dwindled to practically none. I looked everywhere for squirrels. In the bushes, in the trees, where squirrels ought to be, even in a hollow tree where squirrels *really* ought to be. None!

A gray squirrel from Salem

A distraught Peters said he thought encroaching civilization had squeezed the squirrels out. New construction, more dogs and cats, a hard winter? Whatever, they were gone. No squirrels. So I pointed out to Peters that Salem, Oregon, had a thriving community of gray squirrels on the Capitol grounds and at a nearby park, and they could use a bridge to get across State Street to the Willamette University campus. Perhaps Peters would consider selling Nutty Narrows to the Oregon town?

"I'd sooner they sent me some squirrels," was his rejoinder.

I'd sooner they sent me some squirrels became a formal appeal, and the city of Salem responded by donating some of its hardy squirrels to Longview, along with advice for their care. Among the recommendations on how to assure their well being and growth was a suggestion to build the animals' homes high in trees. That worked, and over the years Longview's squirrel population exploded.

Then in 1983 Peters refurbished and re-strung Nutty Narrows and invited me to come take a look at the renovated structure. Then, too, I had never seen a squirrel actually use the bridge, and here was another chance. As it turned out, it was also an opportunity for the town's booster organization to be on TV. That all done, my cameraman and Peters and I settled down to watch, hoping that any one of those pesky squirrels would get up there on that bridge. None did.

An hour passed, then another. Amos remembered he had a golf date and left. Another half-hour went by. Then, suddenly, a lone squirrel scampered up the anchor tree on the park side and, we thought, headed straight for the bridge! But instead, it used the touching limbs of the anchor trees to cross. Shucks.

A few weeks later, Mickey Mouse and Chip 'n' Dale and three hundred school kids rededicated Nutty Narrows, and not long after that Amos Peters died. He and his bridge are immortalized with a nice plaque and a huge chain saw carving of a squirrel, both situated in the park.

And whenever I visit friends in Longview, I always visit the bridge, too. Can't tell—I might see it happen.

OREGON, MY OREGON: THE SONG

Many people might know all the words to *Oregon, My Oregon*, the official state song. And maybe just as many can carry the tune. Maybe even more than a few are interested in weighing a claim that credit for composing the state song's melody was erased by a second wife. But does it matter?

It mattered a lot to Roger Buchanan. And he spent the last couple of decades of his life trying to get official recognition for his grandmother, whom he insisted wrote the music for *Oregon, My Oregon*. Roger died about

four years ago without getting much official recognition for his assertion. The record disputes his claim, but even without documentation, Buchanan's remembrances of his family's oral history seem to support his contention that Nellie Wills, the first wife of John A. Buchanan of Astoria, came up with the tune for *Oregon, My Oregon*.

On the record, Buchanan, Roger's grandfather, and Henry B. Murtagh are credited with writing the number that in 1927 was adopted by the Oregon

John A. Buchanan

Legislature as the state song, after it had won a 1920 competition sponsored by the Oregon Composers Society. John Andrew Buchanan was a jurist with a lifelong passion for writing poetry. Henry Murtagh was a professional musician, an organist, who played theatres in the days of silent movies, a time when the accompanist was every bit as important as the movie itself.

But between the writing of the tune and its elevation to the state song, something seems to have gone wrong, gotten out of whack. At least according to Buchanan's grandson, Roger.

In a 1988 TV interview, Roger Buchanan claimed that his granddad and the organist-pianist for silent movies were not the sole writers of *Oregon, My Oregon.* They had help, he said, from grandpa's ex-wife, Nellie Wills, a noted concert pianist. Roger, at the risk of rattling skeletons in the family closet, wanted this fact known.

Nellie Wills Bowley

"I'm not trying to detract anything from Murtagh," he said. "I'm sure he made an important contribution. But I don't think my grandmother got any credit for what she did with the song."

In a later interview, Roger Buchanan apparently stated flatly that it was his grandmother and grandfather alone who collaborated on the song. But there's mystery here, since they'd been divorced for over thirty years when the competition for the state song was held. And since Nellie Wills was a non-entity in the second wife's domain, it's unlikely the ex-wife and John Buchanan ever got their heads together to produce the winning entry. So Roger's claim seems to be based largely on Grandma Nellie's saying she did it.

Still, Roger insisted that Murtagh's name was substituted as the music composer at the insistence of Grandfather Buchanan's second wife, Madge Ragsdale. A hint of this came in the 1988 interview.

"The second wife would have nothing to do with talking about Nellie Wills," Roger said then. "She was something you just didn't talk about in the family."

If Roger is right, one can imagine, of course, that the new wife would abhor the thought of "Words: by J.A. Buchanan and Music: by Nellie Wills" appearing in the credit line of the composition. If he's wrong, then Murtagh is in the right place. And so is Nellie Wills—but only as an entry in the Buchanan family Bible.

And that isn't all. It wasn't until the summer of 1987 that the state of Oregon and the Sandy, Oregon, school district settled a tussle over ownership of the original manuscript of the state song. Sandy had no connection with the winning entry, except that the president of the Oregon Composers Society was a music teacher there. Dr. Emil Enna retained possession of the original work and took it to Sandy High School. Thus, Sandy pupils were among the first to learn the state song.

The original, now on permanent loan to the state, is prominently displayed in the State Capitol. Thousands of persons are treated to the very score submitted by composers J. A. Buchanan and Henry B. Murtagh…and Nellie Wills?

Tom's Tomb

In a remote corner of eastern Oregon, a most unusual edifice stands as a mark of self-tribute—the burial chamber of cowman Tom Goodman.

It's a long, slow bumpy ride to Tom's Tomb. The guide is rancher Glen Sitz, who leads the way out of Drewsey, Oregon, in a beat up old pickup. You know, the kind that looks like it's all through, but will still go anywhere. So the plan is that when the going gets tough, we'll park our cute little brand new Chevy Celebrity and all pile into the truck. But on the very edge of the tough, the pickup quits.

Our guide then piles into our car. There's no other choice. So stuffed with people and gear, the Chev bumps and drags across mile after mile of lava and sagebrush track, and finally limps to a stop overlooking a scatter of buildings looking much like an old western movie ghost town.

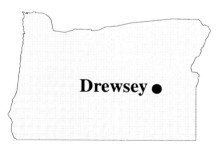

It was a "shoestring ranch," this spread of Goodman's, maybe covered a section or two. Small by standards around

95

Tom's Tomb

here, where one man's cattle usually roam thousands of acres instead of just a few hundred. Short meadow and short land make for small herds. Still, Tom Goodman, big city orphan, dug in and held on.

Some people whisper an allegation that Tom "monkeyed in moonshine," that he hosted large hunting parties and guarantied success, even if he had to do the shooting himself. The least some people say about Goodman is that he was "colorful." Others say he was a "heller." Maybe these people mean the same thing. But no one has ever said he prospered.

One thing Tom might be admired for is concrete. He really liked the stuff. In an era and an area when and where concrete was a novelty, Goodman went wild. All the foundations of his buildings were poured concrete, All the gates and sluices of his irrigation system were made of concrete. "Cement happy" and "concrete crazy" is what some people say Tom was.

This love affair with conglomerate mix reached its zenith when Goodman built his masterpiece—his tomb. A structure about the size of, and looking very much like, a sheepherder's tent. While Tom still lived, though, it was used as a storage shed for tack—horse collars, saddles, bridles.

It cannot be said that Tom Goodman lived a life of bad luck. But his luck turned awfully bad on a day back in 1963. He got shot dead.

Word is that bachelor Tom took up with a lady from Vale named Rita Mary Starke, and he was teaching her how to shoot. Former Malheur County sheriff Robert Ingram remembers that apparently Goodman really got into educating his paramour. Even tied a set of antlers onto his head and raced around like a deer. Rita took aim and pulled the trigger. Bam! The "empty" gun launched a bullet that caught Tom in mid-stride. He fell like a mortally wounded deer. And died.

Ms. Starke was tried for negligent homicide, and despite the fact that one witness testified that she and Tom had argued, implying that was the reason for the shooting, the jury favored her claim that it was an accident. Of course. She didn't know the gun was loaded. Not guilty.

And Tom Goodman came to his final resting place. The land has since been added to another cattleman's holdings. But Tom's niche stands undisturbed, his hillside tomb overlooking what was once his ranch. A standout in a lonely land where few people come to see or care about the resting place of Tom Goodman.

THE BATTLE OF HARRY'S RIDGE

A powerfully important anniversary comes up every year north of the Columbia River—the day that marks the eruption of Mount St. Helens on May 18, 1980. And while the volcano is in the state of Washington, the magnitude of its blast in our own time made it everybody's property. But particularly the people of the Pacific Northwest.

But I'm not here to revisit the devastation and its aftermath, except in the case of one of the sixty persons who died when the mountain exploded—Harry Truman. That's because there's a fascinating story about the crusty old codger. It unfolds around a family feud that nearly scuttled a big honor for Truman who, you'll remember, refused to be evacuated from the mountain during the time of repeated rumblings that warned of danger.

But ornery old Harry, the Mount St. Helens holdout, the irascible but lovable crank, paid for his disregard for the volcano's warnings and people's advice to get out of harm's way. He got a big

Spirit
Lake
Mt. St. Helens

99

Harry Truman
at his Spirit Lake lodge

surprise on that morning of May 18th. The mountain blew up in his face, wiping him and his lodge at Spirit Lake, which lay at the foot of the peak, away without a trace.

Though Harry Truman was just one of many people killed when the volcano erupted, he became an icon of the disaster because he had stood fast in the face of danger, and had delighted reporters with his repertoire of cuss words and his capacity for Coke and whisky highballs. Harry had more than a few cats and a player piano, had lived for eighty some years, and had the attitude that no shaking mountain was going to drive him from his home.

So he stayed, though through the early spring St. Helens spewed rock and steam in small eruptions, and earthquakes rocked his lodge throughout the months of March and April. Of course, Truman just knew that if the mountain *really* blew up, one of those numerous helicopters would dart in and pluck him up in the nick of time. Imagine his surprise and short-lived regret when the whole north side of Mount St. Helens crashed down on him that early Sunday morning. Never was there even a tiny piece of him found.

Someone composed a song about Harry, and a couple of relatives wrote books about him. And the Washington State Advisory Committee on Geographic Names dubbed a promontory overlooking Spirit Lake "Harry's Ridge." Harry was to be on the map.

But one of the book writers, a niece named Shirley Rosen, insisted that Harry was always called "Truman" by friends and relatives, and he preferred to be called Truman. Well, with Rosen after them, the members of the committee quickly changed the name to "Truman Ridge."

But the other book writer, a sister—Geri Whiting, who was elderly but maybe as feisty as Truman himself—contended that her brother was always called "Harry" by friends and relatives, and he preferred to be called Harry. When this split hit the fan, the advisory committee canceled Truman Ridge and hoped that at a future meeting the warring factions could come to agreement on a name.

In the interim, Shirley Rosen leaned toward compromise, thought "Harry Truman Ridge" would be okay. But Geri Whiting stood her ground. "Harry," she said, "Harry's Ridge or nothing."

Mrs. Whiting's stance seemed to stem from the fact that the Rosen book had been published by a Geographic Names board member who was also publisher of a Longview, Washington, newspaper. To Whiting, this link took on the appearance of undue influence, even conspiracy, especially because Rosen's book was titled *Truman of St. Helen*s. The title of Whiting's book was *Harry Truman.*

The issue was still unsettled by the date of the board's next meeting. And Mrs. Whiting, still bristling, demanded that publisher John McClelland be disqualified from voting. Her ultimatum got nowhere. But then she was in for a big surprise.

McClelland, looking a bit bemused, said he would cast his vote for Harry's Ridge. "If it were named Truman," he said, "some people in the future might think it was named for the President, Harry Truman."

It made sense, and in a sense might also have been a diplomatic retreat to placate the elderly sister, and so the board fell unanimous for her claim to her brother's fame. Tears of joy zigzagged in the ruts of Geri Whiting's crinkled cheeks, but her voice was strong and clear when she stated, "Thank you." It was a thank you that sounded a lot like "I've won!"

And so Harry Truman the mountain man and volcano folk hero finally got his place on the map—Harry's Ridge.

CROWS FOR THE HANDICAPPED

Hugh Simpson had a lot of faith in crows. He often stated that they were intelligent, had IQs that made them at least as smart as dogs. So he thought maybe the birds could be taught to help the handicapped. You know, become the aerial equivalent to seeing-eye dogs or hearing-aid dogs, a fine feathered friend helping blind and deaf people.

Although he knew that crows tolerate humans, Hugh wanted to know if they could learn to like humans and, if so, if they would guide the sightless or alert the deaf to a knock on the door or the ring of a telephone, or to dangers such as fire. This idea that crows' "smarts" might be directed to help humans so intrigued Simpson that he went right to work on it.

He set up a laboratory, maybe ten miles west of Eugene as the crow flies (couldn't help myself), near the town of Crow, just off Crow Road. In this small research shop, the domestication of crows got underway. Once they were tamed, the real training would begin.

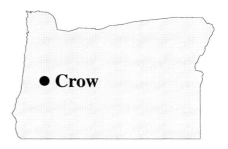

Hugh Simpson and one of his crows

A crow by the name of Junior Darwin was in the vanguard of the research. He was uncooperative. He squawked a lot, pecked a lot, and in general demonstrated he'd rather be roosting high in a tree outside, taunting cats as crows do without any instruction whatsoever. But Darwin and other old crows set in their ways, Hugh said, were not the students. Young crows, hatched right at the lab, were the subjects of the research.

At the very least, said Simpson, the scientists might find many uses of crows as pets. "Believe it or not," he declared, "their closest cousin is the bird of paradise. So maybe we could breed crows for color."

Well, to date there is no crow known to be helping the handicapped. There is no crow known to be any color other than black. And it doesn't seem there will ever be either a helping hand crow or a bird of paradise crow. Hugh Simpson up and died long before he was able to teach the birds manners and a work ethic to help handicapped human beings.

One thing is certain, though, and that is the nearby town was named for the first postmaster. Sure, Crow is a fine family name—even amongst humans.

WEATHER GOATS

The museum at the Douglas County Fairgrounds in Roseburg, Oregon, features a stuffed Angora goat, posed by a highway sign warning of a goat crossing. An Angora is the source of expensive mohair, but this museum display is indicative of something else. The real reason Roseburg's citizens enshrined an Angora's carcass has to do with how very important goats once were to the town.

For twenty years or more, many people in Roseburg relied on a herd of the animals to forecast the weather. Rather than take the word of meteorologists, people swore by the goats on nearby Mt. Nebo, or *pretended* to swear by them. And even if you didn't care about the weather, you could still get a lot of fun out of watching the goats watch the town. Roseburgers called them the "weather goats."

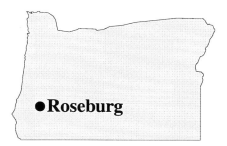

The goats' forecasting was simple. They, of course, had no satellite pictures, no Doppler radar, no fancy charts. Their uncomplicated routine was that if the weather was going to be good, they stayed on top of the mountain. If it was going to be bad, they came down closer to town. And, better believe it, the predictions were so accurate that a local radio station broadcast the goat forecasts. It was fun!

But then, over time, the original small herd of wild Angora goats was infiltrated by abandoned and stray dairy goats, and people began to notice a change. The larger band seemed to be disorganized. Some stayed on top of the mountain while others came down. They seemed to have lost their touch; they were not making accurate forecasts anymore.

It wasn't long, either, before some of the goats began grazing along the busy I-5 freeway, and pretty soon were frolicking on the freeway itself—a habit that got three of them killed back in 1978, with the result that Governor Robert Straub ordered a fence be built to keep them safe. And "goat crossing" signs were put up to warn motorists. That kinda worked.

This Angora displayed at the Douglas County Fairgrounds is said to be representative of the Mt. Nebo "weather goats."

106

But the goats still came to town, casting weather forecasting to the wind, and often still grazed close to the freeway and on one of its main interchanges to the town.

Motorists slowed down or stopped to gawk, creating traffic problems that caused some people to start calling the animals "nuisances" and "hazards to public safety." To reduce the hazards, over twenty of them were trapped and carted off to another location. That reduced the herd to about a dozen.

Those allowed to stay did so because of the influence of the citizenry. People simply didn't want Animal Control to get all their goats. They seemed to say, give 'em another chance. And for a while there, the remaining herd got back to weather forecasting. Top of the mountain, good weather; down the mountain, bad.

But then they took to "fooling around" again, taking fun more seriously than the weather, and in only a few short years their population again rose to over thirty. Once again they began cavorting on the freeway and its interchanges. Some of the goats, now with so much free time on their hands, searched for greener grass and wandered farther and farther into town.

So with public safety still paramount, and maybe, too, because they no longer did the public a service, the weather goats were all banished. There are only a few traces of them now. There's the mounted goat in the museum, but it is not one of the Mt. Nebo animals. That goat is only "representative," a sort of afterthought in the telling of the herd's importance. The only record of the goats now on Mt. Nebo itself is the guard fence.

One can't help but sympathize with the people of Roseburg who so long depended so much on the goats to get the weather right.

Grist Mill Celebrates

The year 1989 was running out far too fast for the Cedar Creek grist mill. The historic old mill near Woodland, Washington, was older than the state, but for years had been getting a new lease on life. It appeared, however, that now the mill would not be restored to life in time to help celebrate Washington's 100th birthday.

The actual date of Washington's statehood was November 11, 1889, and the vow had been made years ago that the decrepit old grist mill would be grinding grain to flour to help celebrate the state's centennial on that date. But now the day was here, and the mill had not kept the promise. No grinding of grain—no flour. But the day was not over! Oh, if only time could stand still.

Some years ago, it seemed time *had* been standing still. For the old mill still snuggled to the rock wall of Cedar Creek, as it had done since 1876, the year George Custer's command was wiped out at the Little Big Horn. But a better

109

Rebuilt flume on Cedar Creek

perspective was that the mill had been built in the year of our nation's centennial. The mill had also seen our bicentennial come and go. And in recent years it had deteriorated to being a beloved eyesore.

In 1980 that love is what set in motion a group of local residents who banded together to form a non-profit corporation, and they set out immediately to restore the mill. This attempt at preservation was fostered by friends with fond memories of the old place, friends who knew that after its early grain-grinding days, the mill had also been a machine shop and a dwelling.

Now it was time to make it look like it had in its prime, to rebuild the flume for water power and replace the works, to return it to its original condition so it could demonstrate what it had done in pioneer times, to keep it as a historic edifice to show the kids and grandkids.

One grist mill enthusiast, Fred Schulz, quit his job to ramrod the restoration. Other volunteer workers, matched by donations of materials, replaced rotted timbers and spent months rebuilding a flume to tap Cedar Creek for water to power the mill. The 1876 structure, one of the oldest industrial buildings in the state, began to look like new. But the work went slowly, partly because of the extent of rot, but also because workers hand-hewed the replacement timbers, taking great care to make them the same way the original builders had.

The last few days till Washington's birthday was a cliff-hanger. The crew was still installing the working machinery, the turbine, bearings, and shafts that would turn the grinding stones. Even on the very day, as hundreds of centennial events were being celebrated around the state, the weary, anxious volunteers struggled to meet their deadline.

It got to be late afternoon, then dusk, then dark. Finally, the stone and turbine pulleys were belted up, and you could tell hearts were beating fast. The mill race was cracked open, and water cascaded down the flume and into the works, just as the first grain was poured into the hopper. And...

It all worked!

It all worked. Eager hands scooped up the first flour and left powdery handprints on friends as everybody hugged and whooped. Again and again, Fred Schulz and Friends president Margaret Hepela chanted in unison, "We did it! We did it!"

Yes, it was grand at the celebration of Washington's 100th birthday—here at the rebirth of the Cedar Creek grist mill.

The restored Cedar Creek grist mill

Worst Food Restaurant

Why in the world would a café be named after bad food? And where in the world would that be? Why, it was right there in the little eastern Oregon town of Hines, and the claim seemed to make *this* bad food outdistance all other bad food in the state. The tiny place that seated only a dozen or so customers was called the "Worst Food in Oregon" restaurant.

But despite the assertion the food was inedible, the Worst Food in Oregon restaurant packed 'em in for nearly four decades. Still, most chefs say their food is the best; at the very least, delectable.

But Bernie Hannaford, who, with his wife Betty, opened the café in 1968, always said his food was the worst, the very worst food in all of Oregon. And why did he say that? To lure in curious customers, of course—customers who wanted to be kidded. At one time Bernie even thought he might open a chain of worst food restaurants.

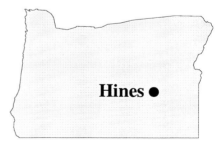

Evening after evening Bernie went to bed with the chickens. And morning after morning he opened the café before most roosters woke up. And day after day customers came in, as the menu said, to "Sit with the flies," or to "Get hospitalized." Sure enough, patrons ate it up. They liked to play the game. Then, too, even bad food might not taste so terrible at 1970 prices: a buck-sixty for a ham and egg breakfast, eight bucks for a big T-bone steak dinner.

After a few bites, diners could send word to the kitchen that they weren't feeling well. Bernie loved it! Wife Betty, the backup cook, and son Gary, who waited tables, barely tolerated the fun. You could say the food was bad, but you'd better not mean it.

Bernie died in 1985, and Betty wanted to close the doors—forever. But Gary talked Mom out of it. He took Bernie's place in the kitchen, and customers continued to come in to sit with the flies.

But then Gary dropped out for a while, succumbing to the lure of booze and drugs. Betty managed to keep Worst Food open, while trying to straighten out her son with "Tough Love."

Gary ran through the mill of despair, joined a motorcycle gang, submitted to having a bizarre tattoo pricked the length of his back before, in his words, "God knocked on my heart." Translation: Gary got religion, was "born again," scraped off the bottom of a black hole just in time to again become the proprietor of the Worst Food in Oregon café. God, it seems, *does* work in mysterious ways.

Gary Hannaford's church friends then helped him work another miracle: The restaurant was completely redone. The designing, carpentry, painting, and re-plumbing took only about a week, something like God's original timetable for getting things done.

But the sign outside still announced that inside was the worst food in Oregon. Also, it probably didn't hurt to have divine help right on the premises.

Hannaford still charged 1970s prices, let his dad's menu-invitation to "sit with the flies" stand. His newly acquired wife, Connie, became the helpmate that Gary's mother had once been to his father. And like his Dad, Hannaford still opened up long before most roosters were out of bed.

Today, however, the tiny haven of worst food stands vacant and wanting, apparently a victim of the bottom line and a marriage that bottomed out. But the building still declares in bold letters that it is the Worst Food in Oregon café. What went wrong? Well, it certainly wasn't the food. Actually, it was pretty good.

Gary Hannaford serving some of his customers
the "Worst Food in Oregon"

Slugs Doctor

Perhaps you've never looked upon slugs as being "big and gentle and helpful," as did University of Washington Zoology Professor Ingrith Olsen. Maybe your experience with slugs promulgated their reputation for being slimy, ugly, and ravagers of gardens. But back in the mid-1980s Dr. Olsen let us know that perhaps we had better watch our step because slugs could be helping to show the way toward treatment of such diseases as asthma and cystic fibrosis.

At that time Dr. Olsen said we should not hate slugs, for it is the cushion of mucus on which they travel and trail behind that could lead to better understanding of some human ailments. Foremost—cystic fibrosis.

According to the good doctor, a better understanding of slugs includes the fact that they are "very sophisticated and complicated"; that every cell in their body has a nerve; that every slug has both male and female reproductive organs; and that every slug lays eggs, some as big as those of hummingbirds (half an inch in diameter).

Slugs survive in an environment every bit as tough as our own, said Dr. Olsen, with skin that's only a single cell thick. Skin so sensitive that a sprinkle of salt will kill them. So, salt is one of the weapons used in what many people consider to be a war against slugs. "That," Dr. Olsen said, "is cruel!"

Slugs have the misfortune to be closely related to the escargot, a snail valued as a gourmet treat. But Dr. Olsen didn't hold with people who would eat snails or, especially, slugs. "There are other sources of protein," she said. "And they're so beautiful. They have the form of a dolphin." Bet you hadn't thought of that.

And, face up to it, human beings secrete mucus, too. But humans have to take a back seat to slugs when it comes to studying the process. In humans, it all takes place on the inside. In slugs, it all takes place on the outside, making it easier to study the process. So the slug slime—so repulsive to so many people who are not repelled by a like slime in themselves, except when it is expectorated onto the sidewalk or drinking fountain by someone else—was the stuff Dr. Olsen and some other scientists hoped would lead to making human health better. And maybe even provide some answers to the vexing common cold.

The slugs in Dr. Olsen's laboratory so long ago seemed healthy and reasonably happy to be engaged in such a noble endeavor, although most of them might have liked to be participants in the project simply because they were offered plenty of food all slugs like, such as the tender leaves of most vegetation. Still, despite the comfortable security of being pampered recruits for scientific study, some of the slugs sometimes became agitated.

"See that one?" whispered Dr. Olsen. The slug was rocking back and forth. "It's scared." Scared of what? Maybe the heat from the cameraman's lights? Maybe from being rousted from a lettuce leaf dinner? Maybe…no, it *can't* know about tomorrow.

So looking back, did slugs lead to a better understanding of cystic fibrosis, asthma, and colds? Apparently not. Today Dr. Olsen says that while her research was "appropriate for the time," it has been outdistanced and outdated by, primarily, a switch to the study of genetics to track cystic fibrosis.

"Two decades in scientific research is a long time," she says. "New approaches change things."

Slugs, it seems, are no longer important.

So the next time you see them headed toward the marigolds, perhaps you'd feel no remorse about salting them or stepping on them or laying poison bait in their way. But perhaps Dr. Olsen would have you remember that slugs are beautiful, have the shape of a dolphin, and not long ago were actively engaged in trying to save human lives.

THE TOILETS FLUSHED BACKWARDS

Seattle citizens of pioneer times had to surmount many thorny problems, but one in particular defied solution. It was one the Puget Sound people brought on themselves by originally building their town on a landfill pushed into a bay. They created a city all right, but also a situation that might have dumbfounded Sir Thomas Crapper and sent him back to the drawing board.

Crapper, the London plumber who is arguably credited with being the inventor of the flush toilet, probably never visualized that a whole city would place its toilet bowls in precarious positions that would turn them into fountains. But the people of Seattle did it—and didn't like it one bit, either.

Twice a day the incoming high tide "reverse-flushed" the city's sewer system with sea water, overflowing toilets and flooding establishments with messes that could best be described with slang words associated with the inventor's name. Of course, the townspeople soon learned not to be sitting on the "throne" at high tide, else they might be topping a geyser.

Having become wiser, though, they also built their indoor outhouses on an upper level, but that meant a climb up a ladder or some stairs to get to the potty.

Well, that problem was solved in 1889, but in such a way that Seattle folks might have been more inclined to put up with their chronic sewer trouble. A glue pot, in no way connected to the sewers, overflowed and ignited a fire that burned the city down. For more than thirty blocks, all that was left of the business district were foundations of buildings lost in the catastrophe. And it was at the level of those foundations that the raising of a new town began.

New barrier walls and great amounts of fill, on top of which the reconstruction mounted, created a brand new Phoenix, still called Seattle. High above the incoming tide it stood, the sewer problem solved. It also created a sub-city which was literally underground, but which was not discovered until about 1964.

Seattle after the 1889 fire

The rebuilding of what is today downtown Seattle and it's Pioneer Square left blocks and blocks of empty caverns and tunnels at the old street level. Years later, along came William Speidel, a Seattle native, journalist, and popular author who saw all those underground catacombs as a "forgotten city."

William "Bill" Speidel

Before long, Speidel was showing people what he had "discovered" and making believers of them, too. Not long after that, regular tours began of the "Forgotten City that lies beneath Seattle's modern streets."

Over the next couple of decades, those expeditions of discovery resulted not only in preserving the district because of its historical importance, but also in building a major tourist attraction.

But in 1984 Bill Speidel was irked. Here he was, deep beneath Seattle's sidewalks with a TV crew in tow, and his way was being barred by "street people," transients, one of whom wanted money as a toll for admission into brand new "rediscovered" subterranean passageways. Speidel wanted to show off the underground area of the Olympic block where just ten years before the ancient Olympic Hotel had collapsed. It was a hidden area he hoped to add to his already famous Seattle Underground Tours. The bum's big, black, menacing dog reinforced the transient's petty extortion demand. So for us to see that proposed new piece of Underground under the Olympic Block, even Bill Speidel had to pay admission.

"Okay, I'll make it ten," Speidel said, "but I need your help." It was both a deal and a condition. The condition was that he and the TV crew be granted safe passage. It was a bargain.

For here among the debris of skidroad residents lay the complete first floor exterior of the old Olympic Hotel, where previously stood the first steam sawmill, an industry at the time equivalent to what Boeing is to Seattle today. Stepping across or around mattresses on which stupor-glazed eyes stared into the camera lights while startled or angry voices either murmured incoherent protestations or shouted obscenities, Bill and the crew finally came to a special spot. "You are standing on the most important corner in Seattle," said Bill Speidel.

Overhead was Yesler Avenue, which in the long-ago served as a route along which logs were skidded from the hillsides above town to the mill, a route then known simply as Skid Road. And so we got our first look at what Speidel proposed to be an extension of what he called "The Forgotten City that lies beneath Seattle's modern streets."

At the time, Bill's underground tours had been a staple attraction for Seattle visitors for more than twenty years, and the new underground area eventually became part of those tours for a decade. But new construction over the years "changed the look" of that part of pioneer Seattle, and the Olympic Block was finally dumped from the route.

Speidel's original "Underground Tours," however, have outlasted him— he died in 1988—as they continue to be a major tourist attraction more than forty years after their beginning.

By the way, something to think about, especially for those Seattle residents whose exposed bottoms are now safe at high tide: A British patent #4990 was granted in 1819 to an Englishman named Albert Giblin. It was for a flush toilet of the design we all use today. Giblin, it's said, was an employee of...Thomas Crapper.

For Love of a Barn

Helen Kling got to be almost ninety years old before she cashed in. And she lived long enough to see her most cherished dream come true—the end of a successful eighteen-year-long struggle to save an important part of her life. An old barn.

It wasn't just any old barn, although you could tell it was as tired as many old barns you see. Thing is, this one was round, one of just four left in the state of Washington. This old round barn was built by pioneer farmer Samuel Laughlin in 1883. Why, that was before Washington became a state, while it was still the Washington Territory and, before that, part of the Oregon Territory. And it was obvious a century later in 1983 that the barn needed help. Lots of help. Just how many more winds could it lean into without falling down?

Not long after the Laughlins retired to the little family cemetery up the gentle slope of pasture behind the barn, Helen's own family took over the farm. That's

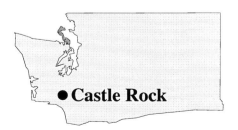

125

The old barn before its rescue

where Helen grew up from baby to toddler to adult. And even though Helen Kling moved away and finally settled in Grants Pass, Oregon, the ownership of the farm ultimately was hers. Anyone who got to know Helen also got to know the reason she simply rented out instead of selling the old place. It was for love of the barn.

Helen's eyes got misty one day back in 1983 when she surveyed the decrepit, aged structure as it creaked and seemingly swayed in a sudden burst of wind. Her voice choked back a sob as she thought about the worst. "That old barn just can't fall down," she sighed. "Just...*can't*...fall down."

Of course, when Helen grew up here on the rural farm near Castle Rock, Washington, the barn was still in use. And on this day, her memories of it came tumbling out in a rush, like they were tripping over each other. Her earliest recollection was when, at the age of five, she climbed to the haymow to see a new litter of kittens. "It was easy enough climbing up there to the loft," she recalled. "But I couldn't get down, so I did what I did best. I bawled until someone rescued me."

126

Helen also remembered horses named Jenny and Dixie and Lady and May and Dickey. Cows called Mollie and Pansy and Vera and Bessie. "Bessie was an ugly old cow," she said. "Really ugly. And she had these funny feet that kept growing all the time, like Pinocchio's nose." With memories like those, no wonder Helen Kling loved the old round barn so much.

But others loved it, too. That love was reflected in people's efforts that got it placed on the National Register of Historic Places. They formed a group called the Cowlitz Round Barn Preservation Association, confident they could do it. One guy even wrote a song about the barn. Calls went out for volunteer labor, materials, and funding.

The old barn after its rescue

But eight years later, in 1995, blackberry brambles were still climbing the barn's walls, sunshine and rain were still streaming and leaking through its cracks and decay. More than ever, it was showing signs of its ancient age. It leaned so far that one wondered how it could still stand.

And then the thing Helen feared the most happened. Seventy-five-miles-per-hour winds tore at the barn until it toppled. Collapsed. Gave up. But not Helen Kling.

"I figured," she said, "if the barn was going to be preserved—resurrected, actually—I'd just have to do it myself." But as it turned out, she wasn't alone.

There was some timber on the old home place. She sold some of it for funding; some of the timber became lumber for rebuilding the barn. Old round barn T-shirts went on sale to further bolster the coffers. Donations of material and volunteer laborers, chief among them her renters Tony and Alex Selander, began to arrive.

Helen Kling's grave above the old barn

The center pole went up, the walls, the roof. People who thought the barn was a goner saw a new birth. So there, three years later, stood the brand new old round barn. Sturdy and brilliant in its bright new coat of paint. Red, sure. Barn red.

And now, Helen Kling lies up there in the tiny cemetery with a view between an archway of fir trees that perfectly frames the barn where, so long ago, a little girl climbed to the hayloft to see some newborn kittens.

128

OREGON OR BUST

They'll call us Okies!" Mom was snapping at Dad, but he just kept on tying down the mattress on top of our car. He seemed to be in a hurry, too, now that it had gotten dark, black even. "Or Arkies!" groaned Mom.

We were going to Oregon, starting in the middle of the night from the tiny town of Gordon in western Nebraska, and the plan, according to Dad and Mom, was to get to Oregon and "start over." That seemed like a good idea because talk among the grownups had it that the Depression had wiped us out. It was 1935 and Dad's small truck transfer line had gone broke, swallowed by debt, I overheard him say, and his partner had disappeared with all the available cash. Dad cursed about that, but I won't repeat it because what you have here is an old geezer writing about what he thinks he remembers as a seven-year-old boy. I wasn't supposed to know dirty words.

"Don't worry so much about the mattress, Honey." My younger brother Grady and I often chuckled about that word "Honey." It's what Dad called both Mom and his horse. "You'd do better to worry about how we're going to get to Oregon with only thirty dollars." That included the seventeen dollars from the neighbor who bought all our furniture earlier in the day.

Although I knew all this, I still had a feeling of guilt, of fear that the move was my fault. You see, Lily Burkett, a neighbor girl of the same age, and I had been caught "playing doctor" behind the haystack. I also liked to fantasize that my father was somebody important, maybe a moonshiner, whatever that was. But I knew if he was, he might be just a jump or two ahead of the law. So, either way, the trail to Oregon was welcome, even if fraught with adventure and danger.

We were loaded up. Dad, my pregnant Mom, my five-year-old brother Grady, my toddler sister Alura, my fifteen-year-old sister Ing, and a family friend named Keith Smith, who was running away from his wife. I never knew why he was doing that, but he was welcome.

Grady and I liked it that Keith had a saxophone and promised to play music all the way to Oregon. We didn't know how far away Oregon was, but we knew it was a lot farther than the edge of Nebraska, and we weren't coming back. Oh, and I almost forgot, our fat little rat terrier Toots was

Gordon, Nebraska

OREGON

NEBRASKA

loaded up, too. Most times she could have jumped up into the car. But she was too heavy, not because she was so terribly fat—well, partly that I suppose—but because she was pregnant.

Then—just as we were ready to go, just as Dad cranked and cursed at our 1932 Willys-Knight car, just as it sputtered and smoked and came to life, just as Dad crawled onto the driver's side seat, just as Mom seemed to give up her complaints about the mattress tied to the top of the Willys, just as Keith tucked his saxophone case under his feet, just as Mom tucked Alura onto her lap, just as Grady tucked Toots onto his, just as I tucked myself in between Ing and Keith, just as Dad flipped the headlights on—there was a sudden, frantic shout, and there in the glare stood my older brother, Richard. Or, rather, he was running toward us, yelling something none of us could hear because we were all shouting, too, because we were all so amazed! We thought Rich was already in Oregon; that's where he should have been for sure.

He and my other older brother, Junior, had gone on to Oregon with family friends about two or three weeks before, shortly after Lily Burkett's mother had discovered our doctor's practice and shut it down. But there he was, standing right in front of us, right in front of the car, waving his arms like crazy, holding up his hands like somebody had a gun on him.

"Wait! Wait!" Rich yelled. "It's me! I'm gonna show you the way to Oregon!" That immediately seemed to be all right with Grady and me because we weren't sure that Dad knew the way. Now we had somebody who had been there and back.

Rich was about seven years older than me, thirteen or fourteen. So he was plenty old enough to hitchhike from Oregon to Nebraska, which is what he had done to be with us and point the way. Grady and I were relieved. But Dad was not. Nor was he very happy to see Rich. "What the hell," he said, "are you doing here?"

Practicing going to Oregon? Author Pat Wilkins tows his younger
brother Grady at their Nebraska home several years before moving to Oregon.

"Dad, I know the way."

"*I* know the way."

"But…but Dad—"

"Look, Rich." Dad was out of the car by now. "Look there. See that!" He
gestured with a grand sweep of both hands, pointing simultaneously to both
the front and rear seats that were loaded with me and Grady and Toots and
Keith and Ing and Mom and Alura and a lot of suitcases and blankets and
food and other stuff all packed tightly together. "Where in hell—this is a
helluva note—where, son, do you think you can fit?"

"Up there on the offside fender." Rich came up with the idea so fast it
was almost as if he'd been planning it ever since he started back from Oregon
to guide us.

There was a short discussion about that; short, I suppose, because it was my opinion—and perhaps Grady's, too—that the only alternative would be for Rich to hitchhike back to Oregon, and in that case we'd lose our escort and maybe our way. Rich had a habit of taking off. The folks called it "running away." But he always came back after a few days, maybe a week or two. Our folks always seemed to be a bit upset about it, but Rich never seemed to be upset that they were. He always came back.

"Do the Twombleys know where you are?" The Twombleys owned some acres near a place called Gold Hill in Oregon, and that's where we were going, the same place to which the Twombleys had taken Rich and Junior that short time ago.

"No, Dad." Rich's answer didn't surprise Grady and me, nor do I think it shocked Dad, for our brother seldom told anybody where he was going when he decided to take off.

"Well…" Dad smiled a faint little grin. "Then we better get to Oregon as fast as we can."

Rich ran around and perched on the offside, the right front, fender. Dad started to step into the Willys-Knight. Grady, I think, began to have visions—and I did, too—that maybe Dad would let us take turns riding on the offside fender, letting Rich sometimes ride inside. As it turned out, even when we lost Keith Smith to the sheriff at Rushville just a short time after we started out—because Keith's wife had called ahead and told the sheriff about how Keith was running away, and then the sheriff stopped our car and talked Keith into going back to his wife, who was going to have a baby—Dad still wouldn't let either of us ride the fender. And Rich never came inside. And Grady and I were grateful the sheriff didn't know that Rich had run away from the Twombleys.

Just as Rich settled on the offside fender, just as Dad put his foot on the gas pedal, just as my anxiety abated that Mrs. Burkett might come to say goodbye but really to gloat—

"Hold it!" Mom made one last try. "I'm not going anywhere with that mattress on top of this car." She meant it.

"Oohhh, ye-ah-ahha-ha-ha," Dad laughed, kind of a chuckle at first, then real loud. "Okay-ay-ay-ay-ay, no mattress."

His long legs hit the ground, and he bypassed all those tight knots he'd so carefully tied to secure the mattress. His pocket knife snipped the rope and the thing fell to the ground. Mom had won.

"We're gonna miss that mattress, we needed it," said Dad, as the Willys-Knight finally lurched forward. Then a funny thing—no, a marvelous thing—happened. We all must have been thinking the same thing, but Mom and Dad looked at each other and burst into laughter that sounded like it might soon turn to giggles, but instead both blurted out the same thing at the same time: "At least they won't call us Okies."

The Wilkins family, several years after reaching Oregon. Back row, from left: LuEllen, mother Madge, Ingaletta, Richard, father Walter, and Walter, Jr. Front row: Nelda, Alura, Grady, and author Pat.

ABOUT THE AUTHOR

Patrick Clifton Wilkins was born in a "soddy" in the sand hills of western Nebraska on a December night in 1927, but Oregon has been his home since 1935, the year his parents moved away from the Great Depression and the Dust Bowl to find a new life for their eight children.

In his forty-year career in radio and television, Wilkins has been a news director, an anchor, and a reporter, becoming a familiar voice and face to Northwesterners. But he is best known for the on-the-road feature reports he did for many years for TV station KATU in Portland. "Kind of like Charles Kuralt," he says, "but with a smaller territory."

Since his retirement in 1990, Wilkins has created two award-winning documentaries about environmental issues in the Northwest, worked as

Pat Wilkins

a freelance radio reporter and newspaper writer, and written his first book—the popular *Somewhere in Oregon*. He currently is a regular columnist and book critic for the West Side Newspaper in Salem.

Among awards held by Wilkins are those bestowed by the Freedoms Foundation, the Oregon Medical Association, the Oregon Federation of Teachers, and the Society of Professional Journalists. In addition, he is an honorary tribal member of the Oglala Sioux at Pine Ridge, South Dakota, as well as of the Confederated Tribes of Colville, Washington, and an honorary chief of the Chief Joseph band of the Nez Perce.

Pat lives with his wife Gayle in Salem, Oregon. He has six children, ten grandchildren, and a great-grandson, all but a few within easy reach of home.

Books unique to the Northwest

E stablished in 1999, Bear Creek Press of Wallowa, Oregon, specializes in publishing books unique to the Pacific Northwest, especially those that capture the life or preserve the history of the region.

For more information or a free catalog:

Bear Creek Press
814 Couch Avenue • Wallowa, Oregon 97885
541-886-9020 • bearcreekpress@eoni.com
www.bearcreekpress.com

Bear Creek Press gives one-day service on all orders
and an unconditional guarantee on every book.